Employability for languages:
a handbook

Edited by Erika Corradini, Kate Borthwick,
and Angela Gallagher-Brett

esearch-publishing.net

Published by Research-publishing.net, not-for-profit association
Dublin, Ireland; Voillans, France, info@research-publishing.net

Employability for languages: a handbook
Edited by Erika Corradini, Kate Borthwick, and Angela Gallagher-Brett

Typeset by Research-publishing.net
Cover design and frog picture by © 2016 Raphaël Savina (raphael@savina.net)
Cover illustration by © 2016 Nicolas Fenix (www.nicolasfenix.com)

ISBN13: 978-1-908416-37-7 (Paperback - Print on demand, black and white)
Print on demand technology is a high-quality, innovative and ecological printing method; with which the book is
never 'out of stock' or 'out of print'.

ISBN13: 978-1-908416-38-4 (Ebook, PDF, colour)
ISBN13: 978-1-908416-39-1 (Ebook, EPUB, colour)

Legal deposit, Ireland: The National Library of Ireland, The Library of Trinity College, The Library of the
University of Limerick, The Library of Dublin City University, The Library of NUI Cork, The Library of NUI
Maynooth, The Library of University College Dublin, The Library of NUI Galway.

Legal deposit, United Kingdom: The British Library.
British Library Cataloguing-in-Publication Data.
A cataloguing record for this book is available from the British Library.

Legal deposit, France: Bibliothèque Nationale de France - Dépôt légal: juin 2016.

Table of contents

Section 2. The professional linguist

Section 3. Bringing the workplace into the classroom

Notes on contributors

Editors

Erika Corradini is Senior Education Developer and Enterprise Fellow. She is based in the Department of Modern Foreign Languages at the University of Southampton, but her enterprise and education activities are carried out at a national level. She leads two National Networks for Translation and Interpreting under the auspices of Routes into Languages. Within the scope of this programme, Erika has created and directed an employability project which led to the production of resources for schools and HEIs, including the publication of this ebook. She has created and developed 'RoutesLive', a webinar series about developing employability skills for language graduates. Her background and research publications are about language history and transformation.

Kate Borthwick is a Senior Enterprise Fellow (technology enhanced learning) based in Modern Languages at the University of Southampton. She is a linguist with extensive experience in teaching English for Academic Purposes in the UK and abroad. She is an experienced developer of online learning materials, an e-tutor, and runs a successful annual e-learning symposium. She has been the course designer for two University of Southampton FutureLearn MOOCs: 'Understanding Language: learning and teaching' (with the British Council) and 'Agincourt 1415: myth and reality'. She is a technical advisor for the Routes into Languages webinar series on employability. Her research interests include open educational practice and technology in language teaching.

Angela Gallagher-Brett is the National Programme Manager of Routes into Languages and is a Senior Enterprise Fellow in the Centre for Languages, Linguistics and Area Studies at the University of Southampton. She has extensive experience of promoting the study of languages nationally through collaborative networks. She is an experienced language teacher and education developer with a PhD in Applied Linguistics. Her research interests focus on language learning and teaching motivation, and transition from school to university. Angela co-leads the Faculty of Humanities research training programme and supervises

PhD students in Modern Languages. She also works part time as a Learning Development Manager at SOAS, University of London.

Authors

Elizabeth Andersen teaches and researches in German Medieval and Film Studies at Newcastle University. Since 2006, she has been the Director of the North East Consortium of the Hefce-funded national Routes into Languages project. She is also the Director of the North East German Network, part of the national Think German network.

Tita Beaven is a Senior Lecturer in Spanish at the Open University and holds a Doctorate in Education (educational technology) from the OU. Tita is a specialist in distance and online language learning, and her research interests include Open Educational Resources and Practices, and intercultural communication.

Gemma Carmen Belmonte Talero is currently a Spanish tutor and teacher trainer at the Instituto Cervantes in London. She regularly runs employability courses for teachers and provides technical support at a job club for unemployed people. Formerly she taught at the Universities of Southampton, Bristol and Galway, and managed bilingual lexicographic projects at Routledge publishers. She holds an M.A. (Ed.) in Language in Education from the University of Southampton and her current research interests lie in the field of teacher competence and employability skills.

Rosalba Biasini graduated in Lettere Classiche (L'Aquila, Italy, 2004). She holds an MA in Translation Studies (Manchester, 2005), a D.Phil. in Italian (Oxford, 2010) and a Master in Didactics of Italian as a Foreign Language (Ca' Foscari, Venezia, 2013). Rosalba is Lecturer in Italian at the University of Liverpool where she teaches Italian language and culture. Her research interests span from literature of the Italian Resistance to didactics of Italian as a foreign language, with a special focus on the use of translation.

Matthew Birtchnell studied French and German at the University of Exeter, spending the third year as an English assistant at a secondary school in the city of Duisburg, Germany. Following this, he completed a PGCE and an MA in Education at Canterbury Christ Church University. He has worked in grammar schools in Bexley and Kent for the past ten years and is currently Head of MFL at Dartford Grammar School where he teaches German and French.

Anke Bohm holds a BA (Universität Leipzig, 2011) and a joint MA (Universität Leipzig, Universidad de Salamanca, 2013) in German as a Foreign Language. After completing her DAAD (German Academic Exchange Service) language assistance at the University of Nottingham in 2013/14, Anke started to work as a DAAD Lektorin at the University of Liverpool, mainly teaching language and culture modules in first and final year. Her research interests lie in language learning strategies and second language acquisition.

Billy Brick is Languages Centre Manager and principal lecturer in the School of Humanities at Coventry University. He teaches Multimedia in Language Teaching and Learning to undergraduate students and Computer Assisted Language Learning at Masters level and has been involved with numerous JISC/ HEA projects, including the Coventry On-line Writing Lab (COWL) and the Humbox, an OER project for the humanities. His research interests include digital literacies, social networking sites, language learning, and mobile assisted language learning. He is currently developing a beginners' Italian language learning app, ImparApp, together with colleagues in the university's Disruptive Media Learning Lab (http://dmll.org.uk/).

Tiziana Cervi-Wilson is a Senior Lecturer and the coordinator for the UWLP and career and employability modules for the School of Art and Humanities at Coventry University. She is a Fellow of the Higher Education Academy and a member of the CU ADD+Vantage Advisory Board. She teaches all the Italian undergraduates modules at Coventry University. She is the Project Leader at Coventry University for Routes into Languages West Midlands Consortium. Tiziana is a disruptive Educator for the Disruptive Media Learning Lab (DMLL) and a member of the School of Humanities International Network (SHINe).

Her research interests include digital literacies, language learning and mobile assisted language learning. She is currently developing a beginners' Italian language learning app, ImparApp, together with colleagues in the university's Disruptive Media Learning Lab.

Raquel Fernández-Sánchez is Director of the Routes into Languages WM Consortium/Associate Dean for Learning and Teaching, School of Languages and Social Sciences, Aston University. After graduating with a BA in History of Art and an MA in Latin American Studies at the Universidad de Salamanca (Spain), Raquel moved to the University of Exeter where she spent seven years teaching while completing her PhD. In 2004, she moved to Aston University, to set up the Spanish programme. At Aston she has taught a wide variety of modules, and has performed several other academic roles, from Head of Spanish to Associate Dean for Learning and Teaching – the post which she has held since 2014. She has been Director of the Routes into Languages West Midlands Consortium since February 2015, and she is also a Senior Fellow of the HEA.

Olga Gomez-Cash works in the Department of Languages and Cultures at the University of Lancaster, teaching Spanish written language and translation and comparative cultural studies. She has also worked at the Universities of Bath, Bath Spa, Edge Hill and Paris VII. At Lancaster, she has been Year Abroad convenor for Spanish students, Language Coordinator, Director of Admissions and Head of Department. She has published in the fields of French literature, European cultural history, language learning strategies and the context of language learning in the UK.

Rachel Hawkes works across the four secondary schools in the Comberton Academy Trust, leading on languages, international education and research. AST and SLE for languages, she is also a former President of the Association for Language Learning. She has a PhD from Cambridge University, focusing on teacher and learner interaction in the secondary languages classroom. Involved in languages CPD since 2003, she delivers training across the UK and further afield.

Alison Hayes is a Senior Lecturer in Languages at York St John University, mainly teaching Spanish but is also involved in the Schools Direct PGCE in Modern Languages. She has long been involved in Widening Participation initiatives and leads on running the annual Careers Using Languages conference for schools at YSJU. She holds a postgraduate certificate in Coaching and Mentoring and is interested in encouraging students to take a reflective approach to their learning.

Bernardette Holmes MBE has been actively involved in advising the DfE during the recent curriculum reform for modern languages. She is drafter of the new GCSE criteria in modern and ancient languages and subject content criteria writer for the new A Level. She has international experience in language policy profiling as a member of an expert panel for the Council of Europe and through research and development of Content and Language Integrated Learning. Bernardette is Campaign Director of Speak to the Future, a national campaign to advance language capability in the UK and former President of the Association for Language Learning. Bernardette is a Bye-Fellow of Downing College, University of Cambridge. Her current research interests are languages and employment, and she is leading Born Global, a major policy research project, funded by the British Academy, engaging key stakeholders from employment and education in a radical rethinking of languages education.

Saskia Huc-Hepher is a Senior Lecturer at the University of Westminster, where she is currently head of BA Translation. With a working background in translation, interpreting and HE teaching, Saskia has a keen interest in professionalised task-based pedagogy and e-collaboration. Her principal research is in the digital humanities, bridging the disciplinary gaps between ethnography, social semiotics, multimodality and French cultural studies. She has recently published on the theory of selective Web archiving, ethno semiotics, and the contemporary French community in London.

Elsa Huertas Barros is a Lecturer in Translation Studies at the University of Westminster. Elsa completed a four-year degree in Translation and Interpreting at the University of Granada, followed by a Masters in Advanced Studies in

Translation. In 2013, she was awarded a PhD in Translation, which focused on collaborative learning in translator training. Elsa's main research interests lie in the fields of translator training and languages, translator competence, translation assessment, collaborative learning and student-centred approaches.

Maria Dolores Iglesias Mora, BA (Hons), MA, FHEA, has taught Spanish for the Open University for over fourteen years. Previously, she has worked in Higher and Further Education institutions in Spain and Japan. Although she is a Spanish specialist, she has wider teaching experience in Language Technology, English as a Foreign Language, TESOL, and Study Skills. Maria has a research interest in Learner Engagement within Online Language Environments and has published in this area. Maria is also the owner and Director of Optimum Intercultural Solutions, a company that offers Residential Language Programmes both in Spain and the UK.

Paul Kaye is a staff translator into English in the European Commission's Directorate-General for Translation (from French, Slovak, Czech, Polish and Hungarian). He currently works at the Commission's UK representation in London, promoting language learning, multilingualism and the language industries, and raising awareness of career opportunities for linguists in the EU institutions. He previously worked as an environment policy journalist. He studied biology with European studies at Sussex University and environment policy at Lancaster University.

René Koglbauer is Acting Head of the School of Education, Communication and Language Sciences at Newcastle University, where he also heads up the North Leadership Centre and Network for Languages North East. René is known to the language community as President and one of the elected trustees of the Association for Language Learning. Prior to his university post, René taught languages and mathematics in secondary schools in Austria, England and Hungary.

Amparo Lallana, Principal Lecturer in Spanish, coordinates the Spanish, Portuguese and Italian section at Regent's University London. She has extensive experience of teaching Spanish and Intercultural communication in Higher Education in the UK as well as specialist Advanced Business Spanish courses. She has also taught in Spain and the US and has published on integrating study abroad into the degree and on students' computer mediated communication for language learning. A Fellow of the HEA, she has an MA in Translation.

Jonas Langner is the German Language Director in the School of Modern Languages at the University of Bristol, where he oversees all aspects of the German language programme – both at degree and institution-wide level. He initiated and designed a final year option unit on language teaching pedagogy for students of German, enabling students to gain various transferable skills and an insight into teaching as a possible career. He is a Fellow of the HEA and co-author of *German Tutor: Grammar and Vocabulary Workbook* (Hodder, 2016).

David Elvis Leeming, BA (Hons), MA, MBA, MSc, FHEA, Doctoral Candidate, has worked at University of Central Lancashire for around fourteen years. Currently, he is the Course Leader and a Senior Lecturer in International Business Communication. He is also a Business Consultant at the Leadership Hub, and Employability Lead for his school. David has lived and worked across the globe. He specialises in researching, designing, and delivering programmes in Intercultural Leadership to teams in industry and in Higher Education. He has a diverse portfolio of professional and academic qualifications. David has published works in blended learning, linguistics, and intercultural communication.

Jane Lugea is Senior Lecturer in Applied Linguistics in the Linguistics and Modern Languages department at the University of Huddersfield. She teaches on a broad range of subjects, from translation, to pragmatics and stylistics. In her teaching and research, she is focussed on the practical applications of language study. Amongst other modules, she leads the innovative placement module for second year undergraduates, Language in the Workplace.

Hanna Magedera-Hofhansl, born in France and raised in Austria, did a degree in French, Portuguese and Lutheran theology at the universities of Vienna and

Strasbourg. After working at the French Cultural Institute in Vienna, she came to the University of Liverpool in 2001 as a *Lektorin der Österreich Kooperation* (now *Österreichischer Austauschdienst*), and is a lecturer in German language and Business German as well as translation. She has published and given papers on innovative language teaching methods and is an enthusiastic supporter of subject-specific learning in class.

Charlotte Medland is a Humanities Employability Coordinator and a research student at the University of Southampton. She became involved with Mission Employable in 2014 as part of the student intern team who designed the first year of activity with Dr Eleanor Quince. Since then, she has trained and managed peer mentors, student employability leads and public engagement volunteers across the faculty. Charlotte is especially interested in pedagogical research, and working with students as partners in Higher Education.

James Minney is Associate Dean for Education in the Faculty of Humanities at the University of Southampton and Principal Teaching Fellow in Modern Languages. His teaching and research interests focus on translation studies and French sociolinguistics, and he takes a keen interest in the experiences of students during residence abroad.

Bill Muirhead oversees Coca-Cola Enterprises' (CCE) award-winning education programme across Great Britain, France, Benelux, Norway and Sweden. The programme is a significant part of CCE's commitment to support the communities in which it operates, and specifically to support the learning needs and skills development of a quarter of a million young people each year by 2020. He works in partnership with a broad range of organisations across the public, private and third sectors, understanding teacher needs, engaging and involving CCE employees to deliver a programme that is of great educational value to young people.

Mary Murata has worked with languages for 30 years. She has taught English, Japanese, and worked as a freelance translator. She is passionate about translator training: she was the CPD coordinator for the Japanese network of the Institute of Translation and Interpreting (ITI), organising training for professionals for several years. Since 2006, she has been senior lecturer in the Department of Languages and Linguistics at York St John University, delivering language modules, an undergraduate employability skills module and the MA Applied Linguistics: Translation.

Alison Organ started her career as a secondary school teacher before taking a career break, during which she took the Institute of Linguists' Diploma in Translation. After working as a freelance translator for several years, she taught at the University of York before moving to York St John University full time in 2012. She delivers language modules at undergraduate level, as well as the *MA in Applied Linguistics: Translation* and the PGCE in MFL. She is also responsible for school liaisons within the language department.

Natalie Orr studied Chinese and French at Newcastle University, completing a year abroad in Beijing and study and work experience in Paris and Nice. After working in the public sector for a few years following graduation, she was keen to join the teaching profession and completed a GTP at Dartford Grammar School in 2012, teaching Chinese and French. She is currently Language College Manager and Assistant Head of MFL, with responsibility for Key Stage 3 languages at the school.

Victoria Pastor-González is a Senior Lecturer at Regent's University London. She has extensive experience teaching in Higher Education in the UK and her research interests include issues of cultural and national representations in the Spanish media, and the use of film and television to teach languages and culture. Her work on Spanish docudrama has appeared in a special edition of the journal *Studies in Documentary Film* (Intellect, 2010) and in an edited collection of essays on the history of docudrama in Europe (Palgrave, 2016). She has also written and published on the directors Benito Zambrano and Krzysztof Kieślowski.

Jean-Christophe Penet is Lecturer in French and Translation Studies at Newcastle University, where he also acts as French Language Coordinator and

Employability Officer. Over the last five years, he has collaborated extensively with his university's Careers Service to design a coherent employability strategy that engages students. This role has also let him explore innovative ways to enhance his students' motivation for language learning by embedding the employability agenda into the curriculum. He is a Fellow of the Higher Education Academy.

Eleanor Quince is Principal Teaching Fellow and Director of Employability in the Faculty of Humanities at the University of Southampton, and a Senior Fellow of the HEA. In 2014, Eleanor established Mission Employable, a programme of student-led careers activity engaging all Humanities' students – approximately 3500 – with the employability agenda. Eleanor has published on Mission Employable in the Journal of Educational Innovation, Partnership and Change, and the Journal of Learning Development in Higher Education (JLDHE).

Marina Rabadán-Gómez is a Lecturer in Spanish at the University of Liverpool. She has a degree in English Studies (Huelva), an MA in Applied Linguistics (Barcelona), and is currently working on her PhD thesis on the development of the pragmatic competence in students of Spanish as a Foreign Language (ELE). Her research interests relate to the creation of language teaching materials and the training of future language teachers. She has also contributed to research and teaching in Public Service Interpreting training.

Laurence Randall is Senior Lecturer in French and Francophone Studies in the Department of Modern and Languages and Cultures at the University of Westminster. She holds a PhD from the University of Westminster. Her research interest is focused on discourses elaborated by European and non-European critics around issues dealing with colonial and postcolonial cultural production. As Faculty Director of Student Experience and Employability, she is keen to promote student's learning by fostering close links between education and employment. She has set up an integrated programme designed to enhance employability across the different strands and at all levels on the Undergraduate Language Programme.

Francesca Rock is a final year joint honours student at the University of Southampton studying English Literature and French. At the end of her second year, she became the Mission Employable Education Officer for Year Abroad, redesigning and relaunching the REALIE website in Summer 2015. She continued her intern role throughout her year abroad as an ERASMUS student in the South of France as editor of the REALIE website.

Marion Sadoux graduated in French and Italian at UCL. She joined the UCL Language Centre as a lecturer in French in 1991. In 2007, she was appointed Director of the Open Language Programme at London Metropolitan University and joined the University of Nottingham Ningbo China in 2013 as Director of the Language Centre. Currently also acting as Academic Director of Online Learning, her current interests are theoretical and pedagogical, centering around the use of digital tools to enhance the process of second language acquisition.

Sarah Schechter has been Routes into Languages East Project Manager at Anglia Ruskin University since 2007, working with amazing teachers in the region who have fantastic ideas for competitions and other projects for KS3/4/5, as well as coordinating activity with colleagues at consortium partner universities and working with external organisations. Previously, with a language degree (French & Russian), a DiPTEFL and MA in TESOL, she had a long career as an Applied Linguistics and EFL Lecturer, Director of EFL, Head of Department, then Director of Language Enterprise at Anglia Ruskin University.

Sophie Stewart, as Project Manager of the Routes into Languages North East consortium at Newcastle University since September 2013, coordinates activity in collaboration with colleagues at partner universities, aiming to inspire a new generation of language learners across the region. Prior to this, she undertook a year-long internship with the *Students as Partners* programme at The University of Manchester, after graduating in 2012 with First Class Honours in Arabic Studies, which included a year abroad spent studying in Amman, Jordan.

Sascha Stollhans studied Linguistics, French and German as a Foreign Language in Berlin. He has taught German in Germany, South Africa, France and the UK, before joining the University of Nottingham as a DAAD-Lektor in 2013. As of September 2016, he is carrying out an ESRC-funded PhD project in Linguistics at the University of Manchester. He specialises in (German, English and French) linguistics, and language acquisition and pedagogy. Recent publications include a co-edited volume entitled "Innovative language teaching and learning at university: enhancing participation and collaboration", freely available at http://dx.doi.org/10.14705/rpnet.2016.9781908416322.

Andrea Zhok (PGCE, Wales; Dip Trans IoL) is Language Director in Italian at the School of Modern Languages, University of Bristol – UK, where he oversees all aspects of the Italian language programme – both at degree and institution-wide level. He has pursued a broad range of interests in the field of language pedagogy, including projects on blended learning, translation, employability and teacher training. He has contributed to a project on peer-teaching Italian grammar which won the Apereo Teaching and Learning Award (ATLAS) 2016. He also works as a translator and interpreter.

Acknowledgements

This book is the outcome of a concerted effort. Its production would not have been possible without the support of Routes into Languages and the community which this programme has nurtured over more than a decade. During this time, Routes into Languages has encouraged initiatives and interventions which have fostered innovation in education curricula across sectors by introducing the development of employability skills, as reflected in this book. We wish to thank the Routes community for embracing this project and all the contributors for sharing inspiring stories in this edited collection. Many thanks to Sylvie Thouësny at Research-publishing.net for her constant support, advice and patience throughout the publication process.

Erika Corradini, Kate Borthwick, and Angela Gallagher-Brett

Foreword

Michael Kelly[1]

"The limit of my language is the limit of my world" (Ludwig Wittgenstein).

Every part of human life is immersed in language, from our most intimate experiences to our most social activities. The world of work is fundamentally a world of language, where people are more and more required to achieve their aims by articulating and communicating them effectively to others. For this reason, employers routinely identify 'communication skills' as their top requirement in recruiting staff.

Communication passes through language, and is therefore determined by which of the world's 6,000 or so languages are spoken or understood by the people involved. Wittgenstein expressed this in his insight that the limit of our language is the limit of our world. People who have learned a second language already understand that there are worlds beyond the narrow bounds of their first language. Those who speak several languages have access to several worlds, and are able to live and work in a wider frame.

The value of languages for employment is not the only motivation for learning other languages, but language learning provides a lasting asset for a growing number of careers. Specialist linguists are in greater demand than ever, as employers complain about the shortage of British graduates going into translation, interpreting, teaching and related careers. At the same time, many other careers have a growing need for people who have proficiency in two or more languages, and are comfortable working with colleagues from backgrounds in other languages and cultures.

1. University of Southampton, Southampton, United Kingdom; M.H.Kelly@soton.ac.uk

How to cite: Kelly, M. (2016). Foreword. In E. Corradini, K. Borthwick and A. Gallagher-Brett (Eds), *Employability for languages: a handbook* (pp. xix-xx). Dublin: Research-publishing.net. http://dx.doi.org/10.14705/rpnet.2016. cbg2016.454

The need for languages in work is not a new feature, but it has become much more pronounced in recent years as work has become more internationalised. Outside the specialist language professions, the need for languages is mainly felt at the point where a member of staff has established themselves in their organisation. Recent research for the 'Born Global' project suggests that languages are not identified as a priority by employers at the time when staff are recruited. Applicants for jobs need to satisfy other priorities at that point. The language advantage comes into play at a later stage.

As a result, it is increasingly important for universities to incorporate into their courses the awareness, skills and experience that will enable graduates to compete successfully for jobs. Many of these are already built into language studies, like work or study abroad, intercultural awareness, interpersonal skills, personal resilience and others. Others may need to be incorporated, such as work experience, project management, team working or enterprise.

The chapters in this book give many inspiring examples of how employability can be embedded in language units or language programmes. Together, they provide a wide-ranging overview of the skill-set that learning languages offers to the world of employment. They also offer models and methods that can be used to improve the ability of graduates to move into employment. These chapters are the result of a great deal of reflection and provide a large number of productive ideas that academic staff can learn from and adapt to their own practice.

Goethe and others have commented that: "The more languages you know, the more you are human". Languages mark the limits of our world, and perhaps the limits of our humanity. It is the responsibility of teachers to encourage students to aspire to wider and less limited perspectives. If we can do that successfully, we will not only strengthen their prospects in their future careers, we will also enlarge their social networks and enrich their personal lives. We may, in the process, help to make the world a more humane place.

Introduction to languages
and employability skills

Erika Corradini[1], Kate Borthwick[2],
and Angela Gallagher-Brett[3]

In the past decade, there has been a growing interest in raising awareness of the employability potential of language students and graduates. This collection places itself within this context and brings together in one place a sample of the many valuable projects through which education staff equip students for a rewarding professional life. In this book, authors from a range of educational contexts come together to offer their experiences and reflections on the skill-set of 21st-century graduates.

This book provides a wide-ranging overview of the skill-set that learning languages offers to the world of employment. Contributions come from practitioners working across the UK in both higher education and school sectors, and they showcase projects in which language students develop the competences requested on an ever competitive job market. These abilities are language specific and also include soft or transferable skills of which students gradually became aware through learning and participation in the activities described in this book. This collection also offers models and methods for Higher Education (HE) staff interested in improving or facilitating the transition from college and higher education into employment by promoting the rewards that careers with languages provide.

Three sections make up this collection, each consisting of a selection of essays and focused, practical case studies. The aim of these two different types of

1. University of Southampton, Southhampton, United Kingdom; E.Corradini@soton.ac.uk

2. University of Southampton, Southampton, United Kingdom; K.Borthwick@soton.ac.uk

3. University of Southampton, Southampton, United Kingdom; a.gallagher-brett@soton.ac.uk

How to cite this chapter: Corradini, E., Borthwick, K., & Gallagher-Brett, A. (2016). Introduction to languages and employability skills. In E. Corradini, K. Borthwick and A. Gallagher-Brett (Eds), *Employability for languages: a handbook* (pp. 1-8). Dublin: Research-publishing.net. http://dx.doi.org/10.14705/rpnet.2016.cbg2016.455

contributions is twofold: the essays set the context for reflection about the employability activities carried out in HE institutions while the case studies give readers a flavour of the projects through which students are made aware of their employability potential. In each section, there is one invited *In Focus...* piece: a personal story with languages is brought into focus in these contributions, hence the title.

We hope that these will be inspiring to you, as well as offer an opportunity for further development in this now burgeoning area of interest.

1. Languages in the real world

In section one, we consider the increasing focus in language education on practical experience either using language skills in 'real-life' situations, such as work placements, or through making contact and networking with employers.

Fernández-Sánchez sets the scene for us by reflecting on her own career in languages as a Spanish national working in the UK. She outlines the many transferable skills which language learning fosters and describes how important languages are in the workplace.

Lugea opens our collection of case studies by describing an innovative undergraduate module which sees students taking the knowledge learnt from a language/linguistics curriculum and applying it to work placement situations. Students are required to analyse workplace communication practices and report back through reflective blog posts and oral presentations. These activities respond to a theme running throughout this collection: the need for language students to appreciate and articulate the skills and knowledge acquired through their degree studies.

Organ, in her case study, goes on to describe the powerful effect of work placements in building confidence and personal resilience. A key part of these successful outcomes is the requirement for students to use their own initiative in finding and setting up their placements, and this practice of giving students ownership and agency over their own work placement is a feature of many pieces in this section.

Sadoux, at the University of Nottingham Ningbo Campus (UNNC), provides an interesting alternative perspective on student agency by giving an account of tutors and students working in partnership to design a suite of work placement modules. The project was conceived in an attempt to address problems in gaining employment in China and involved language students working on placements in UNNC's Language Centre. Sadoux notes that the project has not only resulted in benefits for students – but also for staff, who have received valuable feedback on learning and teaching methods.

Biasini, **Bohm** and **Rabadán-Gómez** outline a high level of student agency in their piece about independent work placements at the University of Liverpool. They report on the high level of support and encouragement that students are offered when seeking and choosing placements, and they highlight the importance of networks and contacts between university and industry as a way of opening up opportunities.

Working placements are explored in **Leeming** and **Iglesias Mora**'s case study, too. The focus of this contribution is on raising the international awareness and profile of students through intercultural work placements. This experience is embedded into an MA in Intercultural Business Communication and aims to develop the students' intercultural skills by taking them through the stages of a guided process, from job application through to reflection and reporting.

Orr and **Birtchnell** pick up this idea in their report on the running of an annual International Languages Careers and Science Fair. The event is aimed at Year 11 and 12 pupils, who are encouraged to think about potential careers and to prepare questions in advance. Orr and Birtchnell demonstrate the importance of meeting employers to gather information and ideas about future careers and notes that the event helps students to focus on their future study path and to broaden their international outlook.

Meanwhile, **Hayes** describes her experience of running an annual conference, 'Careers Using Languages', for schools in Yorkshire and Humberside. The event aims to demonstrate the value of languages in creating opportunities for employment and to widen participation in language learning. Its wide reach enhances the language learning landscape across the region.

All of the pieces in this section demonstrate the value of reaching out to work with others beyond the walls of an educational department or institution. **Gomez-Cash**'s piece on her module 'Professional contexts for modern languages' exemplifies the benefits of cross-institutional working, as it involves productive relationships with multiple university departments and staff, as well as with external local and European employers. Gomez-Cash notes that setting languages in professional contexts is actually about fostering a "global mind-set" and building "cultural intelligence [… and] multilingual professional relationships".

2.   The professional linguist

Section two is about the professional linguist. Contributions and case studies focus on the professional skills of language students and how these can support their transition into the job market. While these pieces explore various language-specific paths, what they all have in common is that they describe projects which aim to equip students with the competences required for transitioning from university to the world of work.

Kaye introduces the context by taking us through his exciting journey with languages. He describes his moving from a monolingual upbringing to a multilingual profession. In his current job, Kaye promotes languages and multilingualism in education and on the job market. In his contribution, he explains the many benefits studying languages has for boosting one's professional profile and life more generally.

Murata opens up the section with a case study centred on the 'Professional Linguist', an employability skills module for language students which aims to develop the skills required to enter the job market. The piece further focuses on language specific professions such as translation and interpreting and related skills.

Muirhead and **Schechter** show how enterprise skills, teamwork, problem-solving and other competences related to the study of languages can be developed from as early as year 9/10. This project demonstrates how languages competitions can sharpen business acumen and equip pupils with abilities which will make them competitive on the job market.

Another business challenge is presented in **Penet**'s case study. In this contribution the author explains how this challenge/competition aims to engage students in enterprise activities. This project also has the benefit of creating opportunities for students to network with employers, thus providing insight into potential graduate schemes.

Randall's case study about the Career Management Skills course for language graduates illustrates how students are trained in managing their career from the start. This work-integrated learning module aims to help students devise an employability strategy when still in their undergraduate years.

Koglbauer, Andersen and **Stewart** showcase how students of languages can gain teaching experience in their final year at university. The piece focuses on embedding teaching practice in a final year undergraduate module by giving an insight into all the activities undertaken by students enrolled in this unit. These include practice as well as reflection on policies and aspects of the profession. The authors also make the case for the development of soft transferable skills which students learn during this module.

Magedera-Hofhansl's case study focuses on the development of employability skills for undergraduate students of German. The author introduces a holistic approach to studying languages and describes the exercises she uses in the classroom to enhance students' employability.

Belmonte Talero introduces 'How to find a job as a Spanish teacher in the UK', a course about how to specialise or retrain as a teacher of Spanish. This case study focuses on the process of developing skills for new a profession and will be of interest to all those who seek employment as language teachers.

3. Bringing the workplace into the classroom

Quince, **Minney**, **Medland** and **Rock** focus on the successful development of support structures which enable modern language students at the University of Southampton to articulate the personal and professional skills acquired during the year abroad – the so-called 'soft skills' such as confidence, resilience and independence, highly valued by employers.

Beaven reports on the findings of two surveys which investigated the aspirations and motivations of adult learners enrolled in Open University language courses. Many of these students were already in work but survey responses showed that they were interested in changing or developing their careers and perceived that the language courses they were following would facilitate that process.

Huc-Hepher and **Huertas Barros** explain how an e-collaboration project involving the University of Westminster and the Université Catholique de Lille has improved the intercultural awareness, transferable personal skills and awareness of real-world 'transcreation' remits and workplace contexts among final year students of French. Using a student-centred approach, they demonstrate how virtual collaboration can help to support student motivation, promote teamwork and incorporate beneficial peer learning.

Cervi-Wilson and **Brick**, meanwhile, put forward a perspective on the employability skills available to students of other disciplines who enrol on Coventry University's Add+vantage language modules offered as part of the institution-wide language programme. This scheme, which has expanded considerably since its inception, enables students to acquire a wide range of transferable competences, including problem-solving, action planning and adaptability as an integral part of their language learning.

The next piece by **Lallana** and **Pastor-González** complements Quince et al's case study in highlighting the challenges involved in enabling language students to articulate the employability skills developed during their degree programmes. They describe a reflective process embarked on by a team of Spanish teachers at Regent's University, London which aimed to explore employability provision within the curriculum, to identify possible gaps and to develop a strategy to support students throughout their learning journey.

Stollhans gives an account of a 'learning by teaching' project in which second year students of German at the University of Nottingham plan, design and teach a session for first year beginners. This initiative involves students on the 'Learning and teaching foreign languages' module and it requires them to research relevant theories and their implications for practice in planning their teaching session.

The learning by teaching theme is expanded by **Langner** and **Zhok** who describe the University of Bristol's 'Teaching modern languages as a foreign language' module aimed at final year students who are interested in a career in teaching. The module combines a comprehensive introduction to language pedagogy with practical experience gained through observing and teaching lessons. This approach supports the development of key transferable skills such as planning, negotiating and presenting, as well as bridging the gap between the degree programme and initial teacher training.

Hawkes and **Schechter** highlight how language teaching can support the development of leadership skills. The authors take us through the steps of the

Language Teacher Award, a competition introduced in Year 9 in 39 schools in the UK, in which Year 9 school pupils prepare and teach sessions to their younger peers in primary schools. In this way, they learn to lead at a very young age.

Holmes concludes the section with a reflection on her own language learning history and career as educator. She then moves on to presenting evidence from the British Academy's Born Global project on current language needs of small to medium-sized enterprises. She goes on to consider the 'hybrid skills sets' likely to be required as a result of technological and global changes in the future and concludes that multilingualism is the 'new normal'.

All the contributions in this collection echo this concluding point that languages are valuable assets in the increasingly multicultural and multilingual job market; that is to say, languages should be regarded as an aid to global communication and not a hindrance. The ultimate goal of this project was to provide a space for bringing together expertise and good academic practice for the benefit of academic audiences. We therefore hope that the contributions contained in this collection will continue to inspire academics, practitioners and teaching staff to embed employability skills into the curriculum of studies, from as early as secondary school into higher education.

Section 1.

Languages in the real world

1 Why languages make business sense

Raquel Fernández-Sánchez[1]

1.   Crossing borders

I am a Spanish national who has worked as a teacher and lecturer in the UK throughout my career. Being able to communicate in English has always been a very important part of my life, and a defining characteristic of my professional career. I started learning English in primary school, and always enjoyed it as a subject, but I never thought that my job would ever involve using English on a daily basis, let alone moving to an English-speaking country. As I enjoyed learning more and more and I spent more time in the UK in summer schools, an equally interesting phenomenon started taking place: learning another language can make you more sensitive to your own culture and can improve your language skills in your own mother tongue. Whether that had something to do with my decision to become a Spanish teacher, it is difficult to say, but I firmly believe the more you study a foreign language, the more fascinated you become about how a language – any language, even your own – works.

In my case, that fascination led to the decision to continue improving my English alongside my university studies, and to spend a year abroad in the UK as part of the Erasmus scheme. I can honestly say that the experience in the UK changed my life completely, not just from a personal perspective, but also because it would determine my professional career. The ability to communicate in English opened many opportunities for me, and it undoubtedly was instrumental in securing my first teaching job at Exeter University.

1. Aston University, Birmingham, United Kingdom; r.fernandez-sanchez@aston.ac.uk

How to cite this chapter: Fernández-Sánchez, R. (2016). Why languages make business sense. In E. Corradini, K. Borthwick and A. Gallagher-Brett (Eds), *Employability for languages: a handbook* (pp. 11-15). Dublin: Research-publishing.net. http://dx.doi.org/10.14705/rpnet.2016.cbg2016.456

I have worked in the UK since 1997, and my working day will usually involve a combination of English and Spanish. My teaching of language and content modules at Aston University, in Birmingham, are delivered in Spanish, but English is an essential part of my work outside the classroom. My current role as Associate Dean for Learning and Teaching means using English in different contexts, from the chairing of committees to the development of university policies or learning and teaching strategies. I know that all that has been possible because at some point in my studies I decided to continue a learning journey that started many years ago.

Over the last 18 years in Higher Education (HE), I have seen many students graduating either with a degree in languages or with some language courses within their HE studies, and I know that the skills acquired during their university studies have opened many doors for them too, as different sectors acknowledge the significance of languages, and the benefits it can bring to a business.

2. Careers with languages

There seems to be a misconception that languages can only be useful if you want to work in specific fields, such as in education or the translation and interpreting sector, but the reality is that language graduates will work in all sorts of different areas, from the travel, media or communication industry to the financial and public sectors.

Learning a language not only develops the linguistic skills associated with the discipline, but a whole range of other abilities which employers rate very highly. At degree level, learning a language will involve a proportion of assignments delivered in teams alongside other students as well as more traditional work produced through independent research. That combination of working in a collegial environment with peers from different backgrounds, whilst showing initiative, is a significant asset in the current job market. In addition, language graduates often show excellent analytical skills honed through the discussion of complex issues in the course of their studies; language degrees will involve the analysis of topics related to cultural awareness, business, politics, ethics and economics. Employers value having graduates who have the ability to present an articulate argument, to negotiate, and to adapt their register or rhetoric. The development of these transferable skills is an integral part of most language degrees these days. Language graduates leave university with a great grounding in written and oral presentation skills: they could end up writing a speech for a government minister or delivering a pitch to win new business for a tech startup.

As with most HE institutions that offer languages, Aston University places a great deal of importance on an overseas placement year. This is often a work placement in a foreign company. Combined with the analytical and linguistic skills outlined above, this vital work experience also provides an important third dimension to students' development: cultural awareness in the workplace. In the British Academy's Born Global report[2], this awareness is one of the unique selling points of language skills and cultural intelligence:

> "[e]mployers believe that it is not the fact that a person may be fluent in three different languages that makes them employable. There is a more subtle value, and that is the ability to recognise, understand and interpret cultural difference" (pp. 20-21).

In a globalised business world, you might argue that English – the dominant language – will prevail, but whilst a new employee might be able to communicate with their overseas colleagues in English, they may struggle to build new partnerships with customers, clients or suppliers. Indeed, data from Aston suggests that students who have spent time on placement will achieve a better degree classification. With the year abroad being an integral part of the degree, it could be argued that a year abroad leads to a better student experience but also to more effective graduate employees, and better career prospects.

---

2. Born Global. (2014). Summary of Interim Findings. The British Academy.

3.   What are the needs?

For businesses, as competition grows, so does the need to compete in international markets. French, German and Spanish remain the most sought after languages in the UK, as the EU continues to be an essential business partner. We know – via research such as the CBI/PEARSON Education and Skills Survey 2015 – that languages continue to be valued by UK employers, with 45% recognising foreign language skills among their employees as beneficial, particularly in helping build relations with clients, customers and suppliers (36%)[3]. Students I have taught personally have ended up in successful careers ranging from teaching overseas to business consulting in emerging economies.

Being able to communicate in a foreign language – alongside the critical transferable skills I mention above – can be instrumental in building a sustained successful career. Together they provide a constant in a world of change. In academic circles, we often speak about, and plan for, developing the workforce of the future – including producing graduates who will perform roles we have not yet heard of in companies that do not yet exist. Businesses and business domains change rapidly, but the need to communicate effectively across borders and cultural boundaries will remain.

To meet this need for competent, articulate and versatile graduates, we must promote these skills earlier in the education system, hence the importance of the Routes into Languages initiative[4] for raising the profile of languages in secondary schools. Universities which are part of the West Midlands Routes into Languages Consortium have created activities which stress the relevance of studying a language and introduce school students to the employability skills inherent in language learning. Some of our events include the 'Year 9 Apprentice Day' at Warwick University, 'A Taste of Working Abroad' at Birmingham University, and the conference on 'Careers in Translation and Interpreting' at Aston University.

3. http://news.cbi.org.uk/reports/education-and-skills-survey-2015/education-and-skills-survey-2015/

4. Routes into Languages is a government-funded programme aiming to raise the profile of modern languages within the secondary school and higher education sectors www.routesintolanguages.ac.uk

Whilst we continue to promote language learning from an early age, and its continued development through higher education, it has become essential to build partnerships between businesses and universities. In order for universities to build cadres of employable graduates, employers must participate in Advisory Boards to set direction, in curriculum design to build competence in key areas, and in providing placement opportunities to grow experience.

It is only with rigorous language academic programmes and with the encouragement of initiatives such as *Languages for All*[5] that we will develop graduates who can thrive in and adapt to an increasingly competitive international business environment.

---

5. Languages for All is a common banner under which higher education institutions offer tuition in foreign languages to students in an attempt to boost language learning and associated skills.

2 Language in the workplace: combining academic study with work experience

Jane Lugea[1]

Abstract

The newly formed Linguistics and Modern Languages subject area at University of Huddersfield sought to revamp our curriculum to embed employability into our teaching so that students could understand the relevance of their subject to life outside and after university. To this end, we decided to adapt and specialise the generic placement module that was compulsory in the School of Music, Humanities and Media for our particular students to service their specific needs and linguistic skillset. The result is an innovative second year placement module called Language in the Workplace. With the help of funding from the Higher Education Academy (HEA), we carried out a research project to ensure our placement module is as effective as possible. This involved assessing our students' employability skills and needs, gathering the opinions of placement providers and employers, and putting together case studies on our graduates' employment experience.

Keywords: employability, HEA, placement, linguistics, curriculum, students, blogs, skills.

1. Context and rationale

Recent comments by the UK government's Education Secretary Nicky Morgan (quoted in Garner, 2014) suggest that the recent emphasis on vocational degrees

1. University of Huddersfield, Huddersfield, United Kingdom; J.Lugea@hud.ac.uk

How to cite this chapter: Lugea, J. (2016). Language in the workplace: combining academic study with work experience. In E. Corradini, K. Borthwick and A. Gallagher-Brett (Eds), *Employability for languages: a handbook* (pp. 17-24). Dublin: Research-publishing.net. http://dx.doi.org/10.14705/rpnet.2016.cbg2016.457

has caused a decline in the understanding of the skills offered by Humanities courses, including language(s). A new discourse on the employability of our graduates is needed to inspire our staff and students and restore faith in the value of a language degree. As educators, we often tell our students that their degrees are not just pathways to careers in typical professions such as teaching and translation, but also that our graduates have transferable skills which are relevant to a wide variety of industries and roles. Communication skills, which our students have in abundance, are vital in almost every walk of professional life. Nevertheless, in practice, we have done little to bridge the gap between our subject matter and its relevance to a broader range of workplaces.

When writing a new suite of modules for undergraduates in our newly formed Linguistics and Modern Languages subject area, we realised that the second year placement module could be improved to reinforce the employability skills of our students. As we outline elsewhere[2], "[w]hat Knight and Yorke (2003) and Dacre Pool and Sewell (2007) both stress is the incorporation of degree subject knowledge with career development tools. [We recognised that] this – the 'embedded' approach – [was] lacking in our practice and [we needed] to work harder to integrate subject area content and work experience".

After talking to our students, we realised that they were struggling to identify or articulate the specific skills that they have, and as a result lacked confidence in their ability to apply for high quality graduate placements or careers. While they could report that they had 'communication', 'interpersonal' 'analytical', or 'critical thinking' skills, they had little faith that these skills are particularly honed in language graduates.

2.   Aims and objectives

In designing and piloting the Language in the Workplace module, we aimed to give undergraduate Linguistics and Modern Languages students a unique

---

2. https://www.heacademy.ac.uk/project/embedding-employability-curriculum-strategic-enhancement-programme

opportunity to apply their language-specific skills to an external placement. Guided by the module's framework and assessments, they would be invited to explore the relevance of the skills gleaned in their degree to a real workplace environment. During 2014-15, the first year the module was running, we received funding from the HEA to assess the efficacy of the fledgling module and to research how to make it as useful as possible in developing our students' employability skills for the future.

3. What we did

3.1. Pilot Year of Language in the Workplace module

The Language in the Workplace module ran for the first time in 2014-15 with 46 second-year Linguistics and Modern Languages students; many of these were students on the English Language and Linguistics degree programme and some studied Linguistics with a Modern Language. Given the rich ethnic diversity of our student body at the University of Huddersfield, many of our students are bi- or multilingual. The module's students were required to find and complete a 180-hour placement with an external organisation; whilst on placement, they were to analyse the communication practices in their workplace. The assessment consisted of two pieces of work:

- a written reflective commentary on these communication practices; and

- a 5-minute oral presentation analysing a particular (type of) interaction from their workplace.

Given that these students study topics such as sociolinguistics, pragmatics and conversation analysis outside of this module, they were expected to implement the analytical methods learned there to analyse language use in their workplace. In this way, we hoped to achieve our aim of embedding the curriculum in their placement experience, and conversely, employability in the curriculum.

In the first year this module was delivered, there were only six lectures delivered in the first semester, and the second semester had no contact time in order to allow the students to spend time on the placement. The six lectures consisted of advice from Careers staff on how to find and secure a placement, as well as a grounding in the theory and analysis of workplace discourse. Given that the students would be in a vast array of professional environments, from school classrooms and publishing houses, to corporate offices, each student would have a very different experience to draw on for their analysis. As such, the online suggested reading list was divided into sections pertaining to various environments and analytical methods e.g. 'classroom discourse', 'service encounters', 'branding', 'linguistic ethnography'.

In order to maintain contact with the students and support them through the experience, they were encouraged to use our our internal Virtual Learning Environment (VLE) to keep an individual blog, which was used as formative assessment. The module leader would reply to blog posts, offering advice and suggestions for reading and research, and maintained her own blog about the module's progress in order to keep students informed and set the tone for the blog-writing style, a skill in and of itself.

Furthermore, having identified a lack of ability to articulate their employability skills, our students were encouraged to develop this through the various learning platforms we afforded them, including the individual blogs and the oral presentations that they were required to do as part of their summative assessment. Consequently, the students' oral and digital communication skills were developed, specifically with regard to vocalising and promoting their subject-specific knowledge and its relevance to their individual and professional experience. Table 1 includes some examples of the kinds of placements our students carried out and the range of topics they covered in their assessments.

Table 1. Placement role and topic covered in assessment

Placement role	Topic covered in assessment
Classroom Assistant in a Secondary School	multilingualism in the classroom

Drama Assistant in a Secondary School	gender and power in school staff interactions
TESOL Teacher in a Community College	designing a curriculum for learners of English as a second language
PA to Director of an International Textile Company	cross-cultural interaction in corporate emails
Museum Guide	multimodal discourse analysis of museum displays and labels
Restaurant Waitress[3]	discourse analysis of complaints and conflict management on TripAdvisor

3.2.   HEA-funded enhancement project

The pilot year of the Language in the Workplace module was largely successful, with just some concerns about the balance of time spent in the classroom and on placement, the teaching provision and the methods of assessment. So innovative was the module, that the HEA invested GBP10,000 to fund a 3-month research project to evaluate and improve our School's placement modules (i.e. not just Language in the Workplace, but also the placement modules offered to other subject areas within the School of Music, Humanities and Media). We also wanted to explore ways of celebrating the employability skills of Humanities students more generally. To this end, we employed a Research Assistant for three months and developed a mixed methodology to gather information:

- Student surveys, employed during and after the pilot year of the Language in the Workplace module.

- Enlisting the help of a Student Advisor on our Language in the Workplace module who acted as a liaison and, in consultation with the module leader, designed her own questionnaire to send out to students,

3. This student used her current job as a placement for the module. Due to financial and temporal constraints on students and the 180 working hours this placement module asked of them, we accept current jobs as placements. Given that they are actively applying their subject knowledge to the working environment, many students report understanding the link between their subject and their extra-curricular life in a new way. Since language is a part of almost every workplace, we feel that there is linguistic value to be gleaned from almost any kind of working environment. Nevertheless, we encourage students to seek out graduate-level placements.

which allowed students to assess their placement module and give a general overview of their experiences.

- Placement provider evaluation forms, submitted by the placement providers once the student had completed their placement.

- A networking event, 'A Celebration of Employability in the Humanities', at the end of the academic year to thank placement providers, build relationships with employers, allow students to showcase their work and future cohorts to meet potential placement providers.

- Focus groups, one students-only and one employer-only, to gather stakeholder opinions on the placement module and the employability skills our students possess, or could be developed.

- Alumni case studies, gathering and producing profiles on our graduates to demonstrate their employability skills to employers and to current students.

In carrying out this project, we brought teaching staff together with Careers staff across the university. In this way, lecturers' subject-specific knowledge could be combined with careers' employability knowledge to produce tailored resources for the students (e.g. ideas for placement environments, CV templates). Furthermore, we sought to ensure that our provision of careers advice was as up-to-date and as tailored to the students' needs as possible. As the above methodology shows, the students, graduates, placement providers and employers were identified as key stakeholders and consulted throughout.

As a result of the HEA-funded evaluation of our placement modules, we made several important changes to the operation of the Language in the Workplace module:

- *Reduced the required number of hours on placement to 150.* Many students reported feeling over-burdened with the module's requirements and quality of experience was given priority over quantity.

- *Increased the teaching time from 6 hours to 12 hours in the first semester*, including lectures and seminars where students could practice interview questions, troubleshot their CVs and discuss readings and theories. Students felt they needed further guidance on both developing their employability skills and exploring the language-related aspects of the module.

- *Made the blog-writing the first summative assessments.* Students reported enjoying learning a new writing skill, and one that is relevant in the digital age, but as the blog did not count towards their grades, they lacked motivation to maintain their blogs throughout the year.

As well as the module evaluation and improvement, several other initiatives from the project improved our approach to employability. The networking event helped us to forge relationships with employers and placement providers. The students who presented their research gave employers and next year's students a better idea of the kinds of subjects that can be explored and what can be achieved through the placement module. Several first year students in attendance met placement providers and secured placements for the following academic year. As a result of the module as a whole, at least one student secured a job offer from her placement provider, to be taken up on her graduation. A full report on the project and its outcomes is available through the HEA website (Lugea, Cullum, Andrews, forthcoming).

4.   Discussion and conclusion

The introduction, evaluation and subsequent enhancement of the Language in the Workplace module has resulted in an innovative venture that truly bridges the gap between the language and linguistics curriculum and work experience. However, in the future we would like to continue to improve the delivery of the module by developing subject-specific careers resources and placement support. Furthermore, we would like to continue to develop teaching materials that explicitly link language study with the workplace. To this end, we are piloting and reviewing a textbook (Koller & Darics, in progress) that could be used in this module and others like it.

One of the key skills employers in our focus group identified in language students was 'communication skills'. One employer even stated that they felt that students who did not develop communication skills were 'dead in the water', and that communication was an important skill in all areas of employability, from the interview process to interacting with others appropriately in a work environment. As a result of this module, students generally showed a broader understanding of 'communication skills', and in the focus groups they discussed various methods of communication in the workplace at length, demonstrating their heightened awareness of this skill and its application. While communication is key in all work environments, our students have also demonstrated keen analytical, research, critical-thinking and problem-solving skills. This module has unlocked their potential to develop, recognise and voice these attributes. Both through and beyond the placement module, we are keen to engender a more positive and enlightened discourse on language students' employability skills in general.

References and links

Dacre Pool, L., & Sewell, P. (2007). The key to employability: developing a practical model of graduate employability. *Education + Training, 49*(4), 277-289. Retrieved from http://dx.doi.org/10.1108/00400910710754435

Garner, R. (2014, November 10). Education secretary Nicky Morgan tells teenagers: want to keep your options open? Then do science. *The Independent*. Retrieved from http://www.independent.co.uk/news/education/education-news/education-secretary-nicky-morgan-tells-teenagers-if-you-want-a-job-drop-humanities-9852316.html

Knight, P., & Yorke, M. (2004). *Learning, curriculum and employability in higher education*. London: Routledge Falmer.

Koller, V., & Darics, E. (in progress). *Language in business*. Palgrave.

Lugea, J., Cullum, P., & Andrews, E. (forthcoming). *Report on University of Huddersfield's HEA-funded project "Employability in the Humanities Curriculum"*. York, Higher Education Academy.

3 Work placements for languages students: a transformative experience

Alison Organ[1]

---

1.   Introduction

A work placement module is compulsory in the second year of most degree programmes at York St John University, as part of an institution-wide strategy to embed employability in the curriculum. As most languages students spend their second year studying abroad, the Languages in the Workplace module was designed in such a way that the setting up of the placement is carried out on the student's own initiative. This case study reports on how the module works and what the students feel they gain from it.

Keywords: languages, work placement, study abroad, jobs, employability, skills.

2.   What we did

The module director holds meetings during the first year to explain the module to the students, and keeps in touch with them during their study abroad to monitor how their quest for a placement is progressing. Students are informed about previous placements in their location, to give them a head start in looking for a host organisation.

Many students are approached by their host university to provide English classes. Others investigate commercial language schools, or explore the tourism, retail or hospitality sectors. More unusual placements have included working

---

1. York St John University, York, United Kingdom; A.Organ@yorksj.ac.uk

How to cite this chapter: Organ, A. (2016). Work placements for languages students: a transformative experience. In E. Corradini, K. Borthwick and A. Gallagher-Brett (Eds), *Employability for languages: a handbook* (pp. 25-28). Dublin: Research-publishing.net. http://dx.doi.org/10.14705/rpnet.2016.cbg2016.458

at Disneyland Paris, in an Irish pub in Japan, or for Camp America. Students of British Sign Language (BSL) often seek placements in special schools and centres for the deaf, as well as charities and local council support services.

Assessment consists of a report detailing the setting-up process, the negotiation of the student's role, an evaluation of the host organisation, a self-assessment of the student's performance, any language or communication issues observed, and the impact of the placement on their career plans. A completion form signed and stamped by the host organisation is also required, to guarantee authenticity.

> "The placement has also given me experience that I can write on my CV when applying for the Japan Exchange and Teaching (JET) Programme. It was good preparation and it has stopped worry and fear of the unknown of working abroad and has eased concerns about working in Japan" [Amy[2], BA (Hons) Theology and Japanese, 2011].

Another important aspect is the negotiation of the workplace agreement which sets out what the student hopes to achieve from the placement. This has proved to be highly beneficial in enhancing the experience and tailoring it to their needs:

> "I went through the form and my aims with my supervisor. I found this meeting to be extremely beneficial in the fact that she now knew what I wanted to get out of my placement, so she could place me in a class that would allow me to complete all my aims to the highest standard possible" [Bryce, BA (Hons) English Literature and BSL, 2014].

3. Discussion of outcomes

The website Graduate Prospects (2015) highlights the benefits of work experience abroad:

---

2. Student names have been changed. All student quotations are taken from student reports submitted for the 'Languages in the Workplace' module, 2011-14.

- "**Sink or swim** - demonstrate to potential employers that you can cope in a multicultural, multilingual working environment and produce great work in the process".

- "**Language skills** - these are hugely valuable to employers and spending time abroad and working alongside non-English speakers will help them improve".

- "**Get up and go** - moving abroad and finding work experience shows motivation, independence, maturity and adaptability - all extra ticks on your job application forms".

Our students' comments echo these sentiments. Many students regard the experience as transformative, commenting on its effect on their self-reliance and their ability to interact in the target language in often challenging situations:

> "This work placement has given me the confidence to consider the possibility of returning to Spain in the future to work as I have proved to myself that I am able to work in a team of people from a foreign country and still be able to complete the tasks required of me without any problems" [Sally, BA (Hons) Business Management and Spanish, 2011].

4.   Conclusion

The work placement module can appear to be a minor part of the students' programme, possibly because of the fact it is not a taught module in the traditional sense. However, it is clear from reading their reports that students value the whole process highly, and that even a negative experience can clarify their career path. The following student's comments provide a fitting conclusion to this case study:

> "I don't regret my placement; it has been an undeniably beneficial experience, even if it was just to clarify that working as a teacher in Japan

was something not for me. But the skills and experience I have gained will be something I can take away and apply to my next line of work, whatever that may be. In fact, I feel that being able to tell a future employer that I lived and worked in Japan at the age of 19 is something impressive in itself" [Barry, BA (Hons) Business Management and Japanese, 2011].

Reference and link

Graduate Prospects. (2015). *Benefits of work experience abroad* [online]. Retrieved from http://www.prospects.ac.uk/work_experience_abroad.htm

4 Intercultural language learning at work: a student-designed module

Marion Sadoux[1]

Abstract

During the academic year 2014-15, the Language Centre at the University of Nottingham Ningbo China (UNNC) worked in partnership with students on the design and validation of accredited work placement modules in the Language Centre. This initiative, endorsed by the UK campus within the Students As Change Agents (SACA) programme, aimed to address key concerns within the University with regards to employability and to the difficulty of combining a UK model of higher education and employability requirements within the Chinese context. This case study will look at the benefits of co-curricular design and at the importance of involving students in employability related projects. It will finally review performance and feedback from the first cohort of students and indicate areas for improvement.

Keywords: work placement, language learning, reflective writing, portfolio, students as partners, employability skills, China.

1.   Context and rationale

Employability is a driving concern for Chinese undergraduates – the job market they seek to enter upon graduation is exponentially more competitive than that which UK graduates may expect to face, as China produces over 6 million graduates every year, 25% of whom remain unemployed (Bagley, 2009).

---

1. University of Nottingham Ningbo, China; Marion.sadoux@nottingham.edu.cn

How to cite this chapter: Sadoux, M. (2016). Intercultural language learning at work: a student-designed module. In E. Corradini, K. Borthwick and A. Gallagher-Brett (Eds), *Employability for languages: a handbook* (pp. 29-37). Dublin: Research-publishing.net. http://dx.doi.org/10.14705/rpnet.2016.cbg2016.459

Graduate employability is also a key performance indicator for universities and of most direct concern for individual schools, as rankings are published at programme level. As the UNNC is keen to figure among the leading division of universities in China, it faces the complex challenge of understanding employability in its Chinese dimension and providing its students with compelling opportunities to develop skills akin to their peers in other Chinese universities. The most problematic area, as perceived by our Chinese students, is the lack of accredited work placement schemes on offer at the university. Whilst Chinese final year undergraduates typically spend most of their time undertaking work placements (which are seen as traditionally leading to future employment within the same firm), UNNC students see their opportunities severely limited by a heavy timetable and by the university's rigid recommendation that such work placements should be undertaken during the summer vacation only. Accredited work placement modules were not available to students at UNNC before this initiative. Not surprisingly, one of the main performance indicators that UNNC has not scored well on in the last few years in student satisfaction surveys has been employability.

Employability requires in-depth local job market knowledge – embedding it in the curriculum demands openness and flexibility. The tensions between global and local perspectives or between academic and vocational paradigms are often difficult to reconcile within institutions of higher education. Discussions across Schools and Faculties have been tenser here than perhaps elsewhere, as changing our pedagogy and curriculum in the face of the big unknown (the Chinese job market) can also threaten our sense of expertise.

The University of Nottingham has, however, a rich history in supporting and developing employability through its Nottingham Advantage Awards (NAA) scheme, which offers students in all 3 campuses the possibility of taking additional 'employability rich' modules and earn a maximum of 30 extra credits rewarded with a special award certificate. This scheme, for academics who are keen to explore novel ways of supporting employability and developing pedagogies, provides a uniquely safe ideas incubator and it is a scheme highly valued by students. It has also proven to be a precious vehicle to bring to the fore specific issues relating to employability in the socio-cultural context of China (Speight, Lakovic, & Cooker, 2012).

For this reason, the SACA scheme launched by the University of Nottingham as part of its Teaching Transformation Plan seemed an ideal vehicle to explore, hear, voice and support student needs in terms of employability and bring them to the fore constructively through collaborative curriculum design.

2.   Aims and objectives

The Language Centre team in China seized this opportunity to improve another area of concern raised by students in multiple student satisfaction surveys, namely the perceived lack of cross cultural opportunities on campus. Whilst the university is keen to brandish its international dimension as preparing students for global citizenship, the reality that most students are keen to project is one of separation between international students (10%) and domestic students (90%), with too few mechanisms for integration. The idea of creating an accredited Work Placement module in the Language Centre therefore sought to not only give students the opportunity to develop their employability skills at work, but also to actively support cross cultural exchanges through language learning support.

3.   What we did

3.1.   Module design

Through the SACA-China scheme, a group of eight tutors and twelve students held meetings and worked together to design module specifications during November and December in 2014. The proposal focused on a suite of modules that would be available as part of degree programmes as 10 or 20 credit modules and as an extra-curricular NAA award (also worth 10 NAA credits). The students (and tutors) received training on how to design modules (learning theories, intended learning outcomes and constructive alignment of assessment instruments) and the SACA NAA module running in the UK offered training opportunities in terms of project design and management to all participants via its Moodle platform. The students' collaboration was particularly important in terms of (1) defining the employability skills which they felt were going to be highly valued by Chinese employers and (2) seeking to develop assessment instruments which would highlight those. The students were very keen on the development of assessment instruments that would be transferable and which could be added to a skills portfolio.

We worked in three sub groups following rapid prototyping design techniques (one group per module type) and brought together proposals (sketches) which were then agreed on – the tutors involved in the project were then responsible for converting the sketches and ideas into technical module specification formats. We used a Moodle platform to share outputs and comments with the students. Our final proposals were then approved locally by the School of International Communications at UNNC and subsequently validated by the School of Cultures, Languages and Area Studies (CLAS) at the University of Nottingham in the UK.

3.2. Features of the modules

In agreement with the student partners, the three Work Placement modules work seamlessly and all the different credit pathways are delivered together as one cohort. The modules all run for one semester – although the possibility of later adding a 20 credit year long module was agreed, it was not initially proposed – and are all structured along the same model:

Weeks 1-5: training phase

- Students attend a two hour long formal weekly workshop delivered by a language tutor, focusing on key aspects of language learning and on the requirements of the module (language learning skills, teaching approaches, language learning strategies, and digital strategies for language learning).

- Students observe learners in Language Centre classes and write reflective notes on these observations.

- Students offer 'language surgeries' to Language Centre students learning the language they are supporting and write a learner needs analysis based on classroom observations and individual surgeries.

At the end of the training phase, students write a draft work plan which is discussed and agreed on by a tutor. Students are free to choose what they will work on, this can be a continuation of surgeries, acting as a classroom assistant, developing resources, etc.

Weeks 6-12: work placement

- Students implement their work plan and have two more tutorials.

- Students are required to keep a reflective journal every week.

- They have a Moodle space available for their projects (not compulsory).

At the end of the work placement, students submit a portfolio and their reflective journal.

The portfolio includes a work plan, a needs analysis document, evidence of the work undertaken and feedback on this work. Students taking the module as part of their degree are also required to present their work orally and make recommendations to the Language Centre team (15 minute presentation).

3.3.   Syllabus and content design

This phase of development was beyond the scope of our SACA project and was exclusively undertaken by the module convenor (myself) working from the module specifications. The syllabus was designed within a co-constructivist distributive learning framework and all contents were designed and built in the university learning management system, Moodle. Each weekly workshop is intended to be preceded by the view and study of a learning pathway designed as a book chapter in Moodle. Each learning pathway includes readings and short video tutorials (as much as possible taken from expert videos available online) followed by quizzes designed to inform workshop activities. One important section omitted in the module specification had to be added: the ethics of the work placement. The face to face workshops focus on sharing of knowledge and experience, on further developing students classroom observation and needs analysis skills and on discussing possible solutions and interventions to issues noted by the students.

3.4.   Work placement autumn semester 2015-16

The first delivery of the accredited Work Placement module recruited a total of 21 students: 5 elected to take this module as a 10 credit option within their degree programme and 16 students joined the course as an extra-curricular NAA option.

The optional in-degree module had purposely not been widely advertised by the Language Centre, in an effort to keep a relatively small cohort in the first instance. It had in fact only been actively promoted to students in the School of English, many of whom opt for Masters in teaching English to speakers of other languages after their undergraduate study.

In the autumn semester, we recruited 4 students from the School of English and one exchange student from the School of Contemporary Chinese Studies (who preferred to take this optional module rather than additional Mandarin credits and had found it herself on the online catalogue of modules). The NAA student cohort was extremely diverse both in terms of degree programmes provenance and in terms of linguistic background, so much so that all the languages offered by the Language Centre were represented (Mandarin, French, Spanish, German, Japanese and Italian). This created a uniquely vibrant multicultural class which had a very positive impact on establishing a community of learning as all students felt they had much to learn from one another.

3.5.   Students' work plans

Although students were given great freedom in choosing the area to focus on and the modalities of their work plan, the Language Centre offered some of them the opportunity to carry out a paid work placement teaching languages in local schools. Overall, the students opted for the following options:

- Language surgeries – one to one or two to one language learning support – the majority of Chinese students opted to work in groups (14, including 1 Spanish, 1 German).

- Additional classes focusing on 'real language', 'language through culture' or closer to students' personal interests (3, Japanese and Italian).

- Teaching an optional course in local middle and high schools (4, French, Spanish and German).

3.6.   Student performance and outcomes

The student performance and learning outcomes across the module were quite variable and certainly indicate the need for some modification ahead of next semester. Whilst the freedom given to students to intervene as they liked enabled some students to work responsively and creatively, alone or in groups, the quality and quantity of their input was quite variable due to their different abilities to respond quickly to the difficulties they encountered in reaching out to students. Some students organised outstanding support for the learners they helped and produced excellent reflections and learning materials to meet their needs. One group of students working on Mandarin surgeries created outstanding pronunciation resources for the students they helped and another student embedded her interventions into real life learning by organising topic relevant outings with the learner she was helping in order to boost motivation through genuine communicative achievements. Most students struggled to articulate the employability related outcomes in their reflection, and their journals remained overall highly descriptive or focused on language learning analysis. It was also clear that reflective journal writing in English created difficulties for non-native English speakers used mostly to producing more traditional academic forms of writing, and that insufficient attention had been paid to this during the training period. Most students also struggled to understand the difference between the portfolio and the journal, and mixed both or omitted to include evidence of their work.

3.7. Student feedback

Feedback on the module reaped very few responses. Only three students responded to the end of module evaluation questionnaire despite the fact that it was also made available to NAA students via Moodle. The feedback indicates overall satisfaction, one student believes though that the workload for an NAA is excessive. All students valued the freedom to set their own work plan and indicated that the independence given to them helped them develop time management and troubleshooting skills, particularly when they worked in groups.

4. Discussion and conclusion

All 5 students taking the module in their degree completed the module and attended all workshops and tutorials. All the NAA students who were placed in schools also completed the assessments. However, the overall completion rate among NAA students was just over 50% with some students having carried out their placement but not submitted their assignments (portfolio and completed journal). This may suggest that for NAA students, having more guidance through a set work plan could improve completion. Module content delivery will be tweaked next semester to include a stronger focus on reflective writing and analytical skills related to employability. Better guidance needs to be given for students to distinguish the portfolio and the journal and it is proposed to create a template for the final journal entry which will be the only required assessed entry for this assignment. It is also proposed to run the workshops throughout the semester to include 'staff meetings' beyond week 5 in order to monitor and support stronger outcomes.

At the end of this semester long journey, by far the clearest benefit of this module is to the Language Centre itself. Throughout their observations, reflections and interventions, the students have given us invaluable feedback on the weaknesses of our programmes and teaching methodology. With great sensitivity they have spoken of the frailty of our learners' confidence and motivation and their need for 2 core aspects of language learning that have fallen in between the cracks of the communicative approach: training on pronunciation and personally meaningful encounters with culture rich language.

References and links

Bagley, D. (2009). *Graduate employability in China*. University of Central Lancashire. Retrieved from http://www.cumbria.ac.uk/Public/Enterprise/Documents/TransnationalConference Presentations/GraduateEmployabilityinChinaDavidBagley.pdf

Introduction to the work placement modules. Retrieved from http://www.showme.com/sh/?h=uDOeOrg

NAA, Nottingham Advantage Awards: http://www.nottingham.ac.uk/Careers/Students/AdvantageAward/Index.aspx

SACA, The University of Nottingham Teaching and Learning Directorate: http://www.nottingham.ac.uk/tld/ttp/studentengage/index.aspx

Speight, S., Lakovic, N., & Cooker, L. (2012). Stakeholder attitudes towards employability in a Sino-British university. *Journal of Teaching and Learning for Graduate Employability,* *3*(1), 26-40.

5 Independent work placements as a gateway to the world of work

Rosalba Biasini[1], Anke Bohm[2], and Marina Rabadán-Gómez[3]

1.   Introduction

The Year Abroad (YA) is arguably the most valued feature of any languages degree, according to employers (British Academy & UCML, 2012). The resilience and problem-solving capacities developed by students who undertake a period of residence abroad are sought-after characteristics in the job market. Thus, most languages degrees in the UK include a YA as part of their programme of studies, and in the Department of Modern Languages and Cultures (MLC) at the University of Liverpool (UoL), students choose between studying at a partner university or working abroad.

This case study focuses on Independent Work Placements (IWP) and reflects on how a collaborative partnership between employers, universities and students provide a successful learning experience while guaranteeing a smoother transition from university to the world of work through the development of academic and soft skills.

Keywords: year abroad, independent work placement, transition, transferable skills, soft skills.

1. University of Liverpool, Liverpool, United Kingdom; rbiasini@liverpool.ac.uk

2. University of Liverpool, Liverpool, United Kingdom; abohm@liverpool.ac.uk

3. University of Liverpool, Liverpool, United Kingdom; rabadan@liverpool.ac.uk

How to cite this chapter: Biasini, R., Bohm, A., & Rabadán-Gómez, M. (2016). Independent work placements as a gateway to the world of work. In E. Corradini, K. Borthwick and A. Gallagher-Brett (Eds), *Employability for languages: a handbook* (pp. 39-42). Dublin: Research-publishing.net. http://dx.doi.org/10.14705/rpnet.2016.cbg2016.460

2.   What we did

At UoL, MLC students who undertake an IWP follow a well-structured pathway with the guidance of dedicated academic and administrative staff within the department and of an employability officer. They liaise to select and advertise vacancies, after assessing their suitability. Students can also propose placements that they will have independently secured. In order to enable them to find a suitable placement, they attend group and one-to-one coaching sessions, as well as workshops on CV and application writing and on interview preparation. Moreover, language modules guide them to apply the above-mentioned skills in a foreign language.

MLC have built long-standing relations with employers throughout Europe and Latin America. This varied pool often constitutes the starting point for students looking for placements. What makes the placements an ideal transition between University and work is that employers provide positions that balance support and responsibility, offering the students the opportunity to put theory into practice. IWPs are undertaken within the Erasmus+ framework in Europe and often with voluntary, and non-governmental organisations in Latin America.

> "The university has great business contacts, so I managed to get a fantastic work placement for Siemens [...] which gave me a lot of practical skills" (JL, Business Studies and German).

From an academic perspective, students in IWPs are required to reflect on their practice and to work on an assessment that grants them credits for their programme of studies. They are assessed in the target language by a YA Project Essay (YAPE) – a systematic and coherent study of a cultural, historical, linguistic or literary theme – or a Portfolio – a logbook, plus a final report to reflect on development abroad (Allan & Driscoll, 2014).

> "I really enjoyed writing my YAPE as I was able to link it to [my] work with victims of sexual trafficking. I gained a deeper understanding of the

severity of the crime in Nicaragua, which then enabled me to perform better within the workplace" (KH, German and Hispanic Studies).

There seems to be a common pattern shaping the experience of most students doing a work placement, which is not far away from the 'W curve' described in culture shock situations (UKCISA, 2013). After the initial 'honeymoon stage', some go through a phase when they are afraid or disappointed for varied reasons. These include the country and/or the job not meeting their expectations, as well as finding it hard to juggle work, study, and living abroad.

At this point, the role of the university is essential, as it provides a structured framework with constant support, at a logistic and pastoral level. This starts with the scrutiny and selection of jobs and continues for the whole duration of the experience. The role of supervisors and reflective portfolios are key tools to help the students understand the value of their placements as transition periods between study and work.

3.   Discussion of outcomes

After initial adjustments, students come to terms with their situation and learn to enjoy and make the most of it. When looking back after their placements, they are often amazed at having been able to work in a foreign country, using a foreign language on a daily basis and having survived and enjoyed the new culture and society. During this time, students acquire a wide range of soft skills, which would have been otherwise developed in their first job, thus placing them at an advantaged point compared to other graduates.

> "During my YA, I worked for a large multinational in Paris. […] During interview processes since then […] I could confidently talk about my work experience and put recruiters at ease, rather than persuading them to take me on by talent alone. The YA […] meant I could hit the ground running when starting new jobs since then" (BO, Business Studies and French).

4.   Conclusion

It can be argued that a close partnership between universities and employers enriches the students' experience and eases their transition from education into the world of work, making them better candidates for the job market. As a result of such feedback from our students and in response to an increasing demand from employers, an industry placement-based module will be offered from 2016-17 to students in the second year of languages degree. By adding the first supported work placement opportunity through local partners, we aim to extend our students' opportunities to benefit from a controlled entrance into the job market, at the same time as focusing on scaffolding such a transition.

As our student experiences show, IWPs prepare them for their first steps into professional life, shaping stronger personalities equipped with transferable skills, an international vision and an understanding of work ethics.

References and links

Allan, E. G., & Driscoll, D. L. (2014). The three-fold benefit of reflective writing: improving program assessment, student learning, and faculty professional development. *Assessing Writing, 21*, 37-55. Retrieved from http://dx.doi.org/10.1016/j.asw.2014.03.001

British Academy & UCML. (2012). Valuing the year abroad. The importance of the year abroad as part of a degree programme for UK students. Retrieved from http://www.ucml. ac.uk/sites/default/files/pages/160/Valuing%20the%20Year%20Abroad.pdf

UKCISA. (2013). A model of culture shock. Retrieved from http://www.ukcisa.org.uk/ International-Students/Study-work--more/Culture-Shock/A-model-of-Culture-Shock/#

6 Work based learning in intercultural settings: a model in practice

David Elvis Leeming[1] and Maria Dolores Iglesias Mora[2]

1.   Introduction

As part of an MA in Intercultural Business Communication at the University of Central Lancashire, we offer a taught module with a work placement that exists within a multicultural context. As part of this process, students must work towards completing two practical assessments, a project presented in a report format and a reflective essay. Our aim is to raise the international employment profile of our students by undertaking a professional intercultural work placement that will enhance their skill set through a guided process, from job search, to a critical reflection, to a final report of the project.

By undertaking the module, the students enhance their reputation by developing the required skills to stand out in the global marketplace. This is achieved by acquiring a high level of employability/enterprise skills that they will be able to articulate in order for them to succeed (Dacre Pool & Sewell, 2007).

The module is structured by delivering two hour-long seminars per week for one semester followed by a minimum of a two month placement (this can be flexible and be done over a longer period on a part-time basis). The assessments are completed during this time and handed in a month after the placements are concluded.

The content of the module focuses on Intercultural Communication in the workplace, as well as the ability to secure a placement for the module and transferable skills that can used after they graduate. This allows the search for

1. UCLan, Preston, United Kingdom; DELeeming1@uclan.ac.uk

2. The Open University, Milton Keynes, United Kingdom; m.d.iglesias-mora@open.ac.uk

How to cite this chapter: Leeming, D. E., & Iglesias Mora, M. D. (2016). Work based learning in intercultural settings: a model in practice. In E. Corradini, K. Borthwick and A. Gallagher-Brett (Eds), *Employability for languages: a handbook* (pp. 43-46). Dublin: Research-publishing.net. http://dx.doi.org/10.14705/rpnet.2016.cbg2016.461

a suitable placement to begin within the first month of study. These content sessions are presented alongside Enterprise presentations that allow students to examine the skills/attributes of being an entrepreneur and/or intrapreneur. These are bolstered by delivery by specialised teaching staff and guest speakers. The tutor also offers one to one sessions and a great deal of support that is often called upon.

Keywords: international placement, intercultural communication, employability, intercultural placement, reflexive learning, reflective practise, MA study, UCLan, MA intercultural business communication.

2.   What we did

One of the key skills we are trying to build is responsibility. The students themselves must make sure they secure the placement. Of course, as mentioned above, they are guided and mentored throughout this process. In terms of the placement being intercultural, we stress the importance of working for a company that is primarily from a culture different from their own. This allows the student to immerse themselves in that country and culture. The seminars lay the groundwork for this but the experience will help them to flourish and really begin to understand the differences and similarities of their host culture (Schein, 2004). Hence, when they enter the fulltime workforce, they feel they can work within such an environment.

The placement terms are agreed by the student, the workplace supervisor, and the tutor. The key is for the student to complete a project that not only prepares them for the challenges of the 'intercultural world' ahead but is genuinely useful for the company. As an example of a placement, a British student worked in Malta on the international marketing strategy for a Maltese company as they entered new territories. By undertaking such practical work, the students often realise that theory can only take them so far. As another student noted,

"I realised that intercultural competency is a skill that cannot be learned from a text book. Even after living and studying in China for lengths at a time before the internship, I was not as interculturally competent as I thought. This is a skill that I developed over time at Bosch" (Student A, 2015).

The students also keep a reflective journal. This is kept from day one of the module till the end of the placement. The nature of the module calls upon a very personal methodological approach to the process. Our intention has always been to ground the work within reflexive methodologies, which was formulated from the work of Alvesson and Sköldberg (2009).

In other words, the students' own professional experiences on the placement are essential. The journal contains evidence of the student's experiences, encounters, thoughts, and growth. The students are the clearest advocates of the results of a combined module that examines intercultural theory with intercultural real world practices. Student B, a 2015 graduate, undertook a digital marketing post in Malta with her project subsequently leading her into a full-time role. She stated,

"the work placement allowed me to take these insights into practice working in a different culture, developing skills, and subsequently securing a job in a very multicultural company. I now work in an office with colleagues from Italy, Malta, Costa Rica, Venezuela, Portugal, Canada, and Spain, so my intercultural education is bound to continue into the future. All in all, this experience has benefitted me greatly, and allowed me to learn a lot about work in general, different cultures, digital marketing, and my own professional development" (Student B, 2015).

What has been fascinating is observing the networks that have built up since the inception of the module. This has meant that past students who undertook placements have now given talks about their experiences and even employed current students. This network will continue to expand across the globe with new and varied uses.

3.   Discussion of outcomes and conclusion

What we have learnt from this process is that we as a university need to make sure that we have a greater level of support for students who wish to embark on careers outside the UK. We hope this module will continue to go from strength to strength. Mainly, we hope to build our international networks so that many future opportunities will arise in permanent work, placements, shadowing, and research; in fact, the possibilities are endless. We end with comments made by one of our successful students; "this experience has given me a chance to think positively, motivate myself and weigh the advantages while achieving objectives. It has made me more confident" (Student C, 2015).

References and links

Alvesson, M., & Sköldberg, K. (2009). Reflexive methodology: new vistas for qualitative research (2nd ed.). London: Sage Publications Ltd.

Dacre Pool, L., & Sewell, P. (2007). The key to employability: developing a practical model of graduate employability. *Education + Training, 49*(4), 277-289. Retrieved from http://dx.doi.org/10.1108/00400910710754435

Reflective journals. (2015). *By MA IBC, UCLan students.* Retrieved from the MA IBC Repository.

Schein, E. (2004). Organizational culture and leadership (3rd ed.). San Francisco: Jossey-Bass.

7 The International Languages and Science Careers Fair: focussing minds and making connections

Natalie Orr[1] and Matthew Birtchnell[2]

1.   Introduction

Dartford Grammar School is a selective academy and an International Baccalaureate World School with a strong, central international ethos. All 797 students in Key Stages 3 and 4 study two foreign languages up to GCSE level (including Chinese or Japanese) and all 537 students in the sixth form study at least one foreign language. To ensure a complete 'learner journey' for the students, from Year 7 to Year 13 and beyond, and to help give purpose to their language learning, the school recognises the importance of providing international and expert careers advice. We have a range of initiatives to enable this to be achieved, but the main focus to provide key information to students, and to introduce them to the possible opportunities available in the future, is through our annual International Languages and Science Careers Fair.

Keywords: international, expert, advice, opportunities.

2.   What we did

2.1.   Initial stage

It was important to reflect the school's specialisms of Modern Foreign Languages and Science, together with the ethos of "a learning community

1. Dartford Grammar School, Dartford, United Kingdom; norr@dartfordgrammarschool.org.uk

2. Dartford Grammar School, Dartford, United Kingdom; MBirtchnell@dartfordgrammarschool.org.uk

How to cite this chapter: Orr, N., & Birtchnell, M. (2016). The International Languages and Science Careers Fair: focussing minds and making connections. In E. Corradini, K. Borthwick and A. Gallagher-Brett (Eds), *Employability for languages: a handbook* (pp. 47-50). Dublin: Research-publishing.net. http://dx.doi.org/10.14705/rpnet.2016.cbg2016.462

developing international citizens"[3]. As a result, it was decided to organise a Careers Fair with the aim of promoting international careers; careers in which knowledge of languages is of benefit or of great importance and careers which are STEM related. It was also important to challenge student perceptions about potential careers related to languages and to encourage gender equality in terms of inspiring both male and female students to have an open mind when considering university choices and future employment pathways. Both specialism departments sought to provide students with the opportunity to speak to representatives from a wide range of fields and to allow students to reflect on their future career paths.

It was decided, in order to focus the minds of Year 12 students (half of whom recently started at Dartford Grammar School) and to inform the learners in Year 11 (who were about to undertake work experience and prepare for mock exams), that the optimum time for the event to take place would be in October. A range of relevant careers were identified and organisations were invited to send delegates, and individuals were approached to attend. The network of contacts available through alumni, colleagues, friends and parents of students was also accessed in order to provide a wide range of high quality representatives, and we were pleasantly surprised by the speed with which they were willing to engage with us.

2.2. Preparing students

In order to maximise the impact of the programme on students, all delegates were asked to complete an information sheet providing general details about themselves, their organisation/occupation, career path, university choice, qualifications, skills and the like. Form time was used prior to the event to allow students to access this information on the school intranet. Each student then identified at least three delegates with whom they would speak to on the day and they were able to prepare questions on issues which they felt were personally important to them and their chosen careers.

---

3. http://www.dartfordgrammarschool.org.uk/

2.3.   Plan of the day

The organisation of the day enabled students to speak to representatives individually, as well as to attend keynote speeches and informal discussion groups. The day began at 11.00a.m. with a keynote speech to the Year 11 cohort at Dartford, before it was split into two groups: one group speaking to delegates whilst the other accessed further input from a guest speaker. The groups swapped after approximately half an hour. After lunch, whilst Dartford Year 12 students listened to talks from two representatives from industry, learners from other local secondary schools were invited to speak directly to delegates. This activity was designed as an excursion for high-attainers in Science and Languages, and also for those interested in pursuing related subjects at university. Dartford Grammar students were then given time to speak to delegates following the keynote talks from 2.30 to 4.00pm. Running concurrently with this programme were a series of thirty minute informal talks on a variety of themes which students were able to attend. The event closed at 4.00p.m.

In total, there were about forty different organisations or careers present on the day, ranging from large companies such as Bank of America Merrill Lynch (Finance), Clifford Chance LLP (Law) and BAE systems (Engineering), to organisations such as Transport for London, NHS, Metropolitan Police Service and the Army, and individuals representing fields of International Business, Education and IT.

3.   Discussion of outcomes

To evaluate the impact of the event, a questionnaire was completed by both students and delegates. Local schools provided positive feedback and the vast majority of delegates thought it to be a "purposeful, informative and well organised" opportunity. Of central importance to this success was the pre-event preparation with students, which enabled them to be well informed and focussed on what they, as individuals, wanted to achieve from the day. This preparation was also appreciated by the delegates who praised the open mindedness of the students, together with their exemplary behaviour, excellent attitude and carefully targeted questions.

Student feedback showed that the delegates chosen represented the majority of the careers in which they were interested, and provided them with essential information which they needed to reinforce or reshape their choices. Significantly, the feedback also identified the students' increased awareness of the prominence of language ability in many of their career choices. Many students felt encouraged to continue to study a language at university level through a combined degree and the event raised awareness of the benefits of being able to speak a second or third language when applying for employment, particularly with international companies.

As organisers of the event, we feel that there are still further opportunities remaining to develop the expertise provided by the alumni network to promote careers in science and language subjects, as well as more generally developing the range of careers/organisations represented. We would also like to increase the number of students from other schools who are able to access the event.

4.   Conclusion

A key aim of the International Science and Languages Careers Fair is to broaden the students' international outlook in terms of future study and career choices. Dartford Grammar School is confident that this objective has been successfully achieved and that the provision of expert advice has been strengthened through this event. A continuing aim will be to ensure that delegates return each year. For this to happen, delegates must appreciate that the school is dedicated to investing serious effort and valuable time to the careers' advice provided by the school.

Reference and link

Dartford grammar school: http://www.dartfordgrammarschool.org.uk/

8 Careers Using Languages: how to set up a conference for schools

Alison Hayes[1]

1.   Introduction

Since 2011, York St John University (YSJU) has run an annual one-day 'Careers using Languages' conference for schools in Yorkshire and Humberside. It has the aim of demonstrating to school students the opportunities in life that speaking a foreign language opens up as well as showing how they will be able to offer an added bonus to their future employers if they maintain their language skills.

The conference programme includes a high-profile keynote speaker with wide experience of using languages in their career, while the rest of the day comprises a range of interactive workshops.

It is advertised to local schools, including those with a high Index of Multiple Deprivation (IMD) score, and their feedback has always been overwhelmingly positive.

So far the event has been funded by Routes into Languages and supported by York St John Business School, and has become a fixture of our Widening Participation (WP) activities.

Keywords: languages, careers, schools, employability.

1. York St John University, York, United Kingdom; A.Hayes@yorksj.ac.uk

How to cite this chapter: Hayes, A. (2016). Careers Using Languages: how to set up a conference for schools. In E. Corradini, K. Borthwick and A. Gallagher-Brett (Eds), *Employability for languages: a handbook* (pp. 51-55). Dublin: Research-publishing.net. http://dx.doi.org/10.14705/rpnet.2016.cbg2016.463

2.   What we do

"Close to half of businesses (45%) recognise foreign language skills among their employees as beneficial" (CBI, 2015, p. 7).

Primarily, the Careers using Languages event aims to convey to school students the message that having some language skills will increase the variety and the level of jobs available to them, even if languages are not the main focus of their job or career, hence the title of the event: not Careers in Languages but Careers using Languages.

The students who attend are mainly in Years 9 and 10, usually between 13 and 16 years old, and typically are studying one or more languages at school. It is hoped that they will be inspired and motivated by the event to continue studying languages at A-level and beyond, and that in the future they will be aware of and interested in the possibilities that languages can create.

Engaging keynote speakers who have a career in an industry other than the obvious language-based areas of teaching, translating and interpreting are invited. An example is Sally Fagan of Business Language Champions (http://business-language-champions.co.uk/), who has an impressive background in international sales. She explained how she was employed because of her languages and trained in engineering and sales by her employers, as they felt this would be far quicker than employing an engineer and training them in languages. The keynote speaker for the 2015 conference was a representative from the Government Communications Headquarters (GCHQ), who explained to students how languages can be useful in the world of James Bond!

The parallel sessions which comprise the rest of the day are mainly interactive; for example, getting students to create a French or Spanish marketing campaign, how languages are used in the hospitality industry, volunteering abroad, using culture and body-language when communicating internationally, studying abroad, language and culture tasters in Japanese, Arabic and British Sign Language, and also a hands-on introduction to interpreting.

"There is value in language learning for students of all disciplines and for individuals of all ages, throughout life" (Born Global Symposium, 2014, p. 36).

In addition, the event gives students a taste of university life: the chance to see that it is a welcoming, lively place, and they are able to meet and ask questions to current undergraduate students in the form of Student Ambassadors, including during an optional tour of the campus at the end of the day, when students can see the range of facilities on offer.

The event has been funded by Routes into Languages for the last five years, and publicised to schools throughout the region, particularly those with a high IMD score, as this is the purpose of Routes into Languages: to encourage participation in Higher Education (HE) from schools with low involvement. These are the students who can often benefit most from the breaking down of perceived barriers or misconceptions about HE through a day of inspiring language and culture events in a university environment.

3.   Discussion of outcomes

Feedback from staff and students after each event has been overwhelmingly positive:

"All lectures and taster sessions were well planned and well delivered. Found the opening lecture interesting as to the roles in industry having a language can benefit", said one teacher, and student comments included: "I really enjoyed this event, it has made me look further into studying languages"; "Motivated my thinking about languages and my future"; "I would like more opportunities in the future to do events like this" (Routes into Languages, 2015, p. 1).

While YSJU has often been involved in running taster sessions or masterclasses on school premises, it is also important to hold events at YSJU, in order to give students a taste of HE as well as input on careers. Events have also been run on campus comprising language tasters and an 'Introduction to HE talk by the marketing department, but these tended to involve one school at a time. The Careers using Languages conference involves students from five or six different schools, and while students tend to remain within their school groups, it is beneficial for them to see others from different institutions and possibly observe different attitudes to languages and careers amongst their peers.

4. Conclusion

Although Routes into Languages funding is coming to an end, YSJU intends to continue to hold the conference using funding from other sources. As this event has become a regular part of the YSJU Business School's WP activities, hopefully it will endure and evolve for many years to come. The Born Global Symposium's Interim Report states that:

> "Young people who can connect with others through their languages and through a shared understanding of diverse cultures are at an advantage in the global labour market over their monolingual peers" (The British Academy, 2014, p. 21).

The Languages team at YSJU hope that in a small way their event contributes to this.

References and links

Born Global Symposium. (2014). *Summary of interim findings*. Retrieved from http://www. ucml.ac.uk/sites/default/files/shapingthefuture/101/Born%20Global_Summary%20 of%20Interim%20Findings%2017%20Oct%202014(1).pdf

CBI. (2015). *Inspiring growth: CBI/Pearson Education and Skills Survey 2015* [online]. London: Confederation of British Industry. Retrieved from http://news.cbi.org.uk/reports/ education-and-skills-survey-2015/education-and-skills-survey-2015/

Routes into Languages. (2015). *Careers using languages* [online]. York St John University. Retrieved from http://goo.gl/0nt2jc

The British Academy. (2014). *Born global: summary of interim findings* [online]. London: The British Academy. Retrieved from http://www.britac.ac.uk/policy/Born_Global.cfm

9 'Professional Contexts for Modern Languages': work experience and academic reflection in a multilingual context

Olga Gomez-Cash[1]

Abstract

In the second year module 'Professional Contexts for Modern Languages' at Lancaster University, students take 20-25 hour placements, and using a multimodal forum, they articulate their challenges, development and understanding of the varying contexts in which they are working. In summative assessment, students across languages and types of activity communicate and learn from each other so as to foster a broad, cross cultural understanding of language-based professional and business contexts (mainly in educational, digital marketing and translation sectors both in the UK and abroad). The module establishes a mutually productive engagement between a university languages department, faculty employability and central careers staff, the Lancaster University Students Union (that source teaching placements) and local and European employers. Inspired by a vision of modern languages degrees as fostering a global mind-set and cultural intelligence, the course allows us to rethink language learning within a framework of skills for employability.

Keywords: skills development, business contexts, cultural intelligence, student placements, multilingual contexts.

1. Lancaster University, Lancaster, United Kingdom; o.gomez@lancaster.ac.uk

How to cite this chapter: Gomez-Cash, O. (2016). 'Professional Contexts for Modern Languages': work experience and academic reflection in a multilingual context. In E. Corradini, K. Borthwick and A. Gallagher-Brett (Eds), *Employability for languages: a handbook* (pp. 57-66). Dublin: Research-publishing.net. http://dx.doi.org/10.14705/rpnet.2016.cbg2016.464

1.   Context and rationale

Admissions tutors and others who promote studying languages degrees often repeat that language graduates develop a broad range of transferable skills, such as a capacity to deal with people across cultural boundaries, giving them an advantage in the job market. Colleagues who oversee year abroad placements are sure of this too. Language professionals often cite the multilingual nature of contemporary global societies we live in to underscore the importance of language degrees. Much of this discourse refers to by-products of studying languages.

I had participated in a faculty-wide project (Dawes, Fox, & Gomez-Cash, 2016) focused on the ways in which employability can be integrated into the curriculum. A central principle of the project was a sense of the importance of a subject-specific approach to employability, although we started by considering institutional guidelines on employability and engagement as overarching strategic goals. Employability has of course been defined in our institution, but how it is to be embedded is not explicit. It also became one of our goals to explore ways of expanding notions of employability beyond Destinations of Leavers from Higher Education (DELHE) statistics.

Several employability skills models were reviewed in order to identify 'common' skills across these. Using Cole and Tibby's (2013) Higher Education Authority document 'Defining and developing your approach to employability', we identified employability models such as the CBI and NUS (2011) framework. In addition, we referred to the Lancaster University's skills bank which is used by our Careers Service to highlight the employability skills graduates need to develop. We also considered Jones and Warnock's (2014) competency framework for student work based learning. The skills and competencies identified in these models were mapped onto an employability skills matrix in order to identify commonly occurring skills. We blended the findings with a mapping exercise of the generic skills identified in Quality Assurance Agency's benchmark statements for Humanities disciplines. As a modern linguist, it was reassuring that the general discourse about language degrees is entirely accurate and that of the skills that humanities degrees aim to foster, language degrees offer the broadest array of skills.

The employability skills that featured most prominently were:

- communication skills (verbal and written);

- problem-solving;

- team-work;

- self-management;

- computer literacy/IT skills;

- business/commercial awareness;

- numeracy.

Other related skills were:

- adaptability/flexibility;

- ability to work independently;

- decision making;

- planning and organising;

- initiative taking;

- creativity;

- leadership skills;

- self-awareness;

- analytical/evaluation skills;

- networking;

- cultural sensitivity.

Part of the faculty project was to run a workshop with employers and recent alumni which was firstly designed to interrogate what employers looked for in graduates and secondly, if the skills included in our matrix were the type of skills employers were looking for in graduates. Employer satisfaction was generally high except perhaps in business and customer awareness, a finding similar to that reported in the CBI/Pearson Education and Skills survey (2014). Two skills that are common across the majority of employability skills models but are given little or no importance in the Humanities subject benchmarks are indeed business/commercial awareness and numeracy.

The matter of business awareness may seem a problematic one for a humanities subject: are we expecting to deliver courses looking at individual national contexts and the economy, business, accounting, law and the marketplace? A more productive approach seemed to be to focus on understanding the context that our discipline operates in and how that discipline 'changes shape' when explored via this professional context.

A 'Professional Contexts' approach, therefore, would support students to begin to appreciate and explore, as part of their reflective work placement reports, the financial, business and language policy context of the placements in, for example, local school, commercial language-teaching companies, translation companies, and digital marketing. There are many debates for them to start to engage with, for example, to name a few: what is the status of languages in current educational policy in the UK and abroad? How do professional translators work with translation software? How do multilingual companies engage with various languages? What are the challenges for multilingual practice in the digital era? What are the challenges for private language schools?

2.   Aims and objectives

One of my aims in developing a 'Professional Contexts for Modern Languages' course for second year undergraduates on language and joint language with non-language subject degrees at Lancaster University was to create a course in which skills development via work experience in a multilingual context would be central and indeed, the object of academic reflection.

Developing skills that are valued in the workplace while at university can support an engaged and proactive transition into employment upon graduation. My department of European Languages and Cultures already has a consistent track record of success with regards to graduate employment. It seemed important, institutionally, as mentioned above, to have an academic space that enhanced awareness of this aspect of our languages degrees and supported students to explicitly articulate their development of skills and attributes that enhance employability.

There are also contextual matters of importance to languages that needed to be embedded in the design of the course itself. These are very clearly delineated in the *Born Global* interim findings (British Academy, 2014), which I will briefly summarise here. Facing head-on the issues of subject identity for languages as a subject (is it an academic discipline or skill?), and given the importance of employability and the interrelatedness of mobility and multilingualism, the report asks a crucial question: can languages be located within a broader matrix of transferable skills? Employers interviewed for Born Global were convinced of the importance of commercial awareness and work experience, in particular applying language skills in 'real world' contexts. Employer satisfaction was generally low for language skills, intercultural awareness as well as business and customer awareness. These skills are all classified as employability skills for graduates and this makes the connection between languages and employability a fertile one.

This report's vision of modern languages degrees as fostering a global mind-set and cultural intelligence is an inspiring one. It seemed urgent to forge a module where students were required to develop the skills and attributes that prepare them for multilingual employment and explore their development of linguistic fluency in the target language in a professional context. Following on from this, it seems such a module would also enhance a student's ability to recognise and interpret cultural codes of practice and 'translanguage', and take the first steps in learning to build multilingual professional relationships.

3.   What we did

One of Lancaster's innovations in language degrees is the successful development of comparative courses that straddle different languages and create coherence by promoting an understanding of European cultures and societies within a global context.

Our second year comparative courses, taken by all students who are on a joint or single major in a language or languages, allow the students to take wide-ranging courses on the following themes: Language and identity, European economic history, Comparative literature, Cultural theory, and Comparative film studies. The Professional context module became another option amongst these comparative modules. It is a strength then of this module that it is taken by students across languages and this further emphasises the need to make comparisons across a variety of national and linguistic contexts of employment.

In order to formalise the process of taking the module and to start developing our students professionally, short interviews were held in the weeks leading up to module enrolment as well as part of the sourcing of placements.

The Faculty of Arts and Social Sciences has been creating a bank of generic unpaid work placements to be offered across the faculty for some years. These placements are designed to enhance student employability, but they are also designed to develop an enhanced engagement between our degree schemes (across all our subject areas) and the local business community. The work of sourcing placements, sometimes by the student, languages staff, or the faculty placement officer, is part of the process of engagement and discovery – which local companies can we work with? Which European companies can we work with to find short placements?

The preparation for the module, i.e. the process of preparing and sending CVs, going through Disclosure and Barring Services (DBS) checks, entering in communication with the professionals that they will work with, etc. is already part of the learning and skills development process.

As part of the course, students typically spend between 25-30 hours over a period of 10 weeks engaging with a placement organisation in the second part of the second year. Alternatively, students may undertake a 'block' placement over a two to three week period during the Easter vacation. This option allows students to undertake placements abroad and to work with companies that we have created partnerships with for the Year Abroad.

Students undertaking school placements do so under the auspices of an engagement initiative undertaken by our Students' Union (SU). They thus undertake a volunteer evening training event dealing with issues such as lesson planning, safeguarding and protection during which they engage with professional staff in the SU and teachers from local schools. The SU also finances checks.

The academic reflection begins in two seminars at the start of the course by getting students to use self-evaluation tools to become aware of their starting point. Online psychometric testing is available via the University Careers service. Although the tests are done in English, the software does provide some alternatives in the languages we deliver at Lancaster (French, German, Italian and Spanish). This is a first step in identifying the attributes they have and those which they need to develop. A self-audit of the key skills that students should be developing through their degree provides another tool in which students can start to articulate their development needs in an e-portfolio. A workshop on employability skills led by University Careers staff allows students to articulate their findings from the tools exploring their attributes, skills and readiness for employability and discuss these with each other. Students are encouraged to take an array of central career development workshops (on using LinkedIn, on networking...) and reflect on them.

Alongside their placements, formative assessment in the shape of an e-log book encourages students to gather up these reflections and articulate their development and understanding of the varying business and policy contexts they are working in. Using this multimodal forum, students develop narratives and visualisations of working in a language based context that explore and reinforce the skills they have identified they need to develop. In one mid-term session, formative feedback is also provided on initial drafts of and ideas for the reflective report. My experience is that this is the most difficult part for the students, and that support is needed for them to able to frame their experience in a context and 'theorise' it.

The project report asks students to explore a maximum of three features of the business and policy contexts they worked in. They can reflect on working in and with languages, and related cross-cultural issues assess issues of communicating across cultures/languages and critically reflect on how their linguistic and cultural knowledge can be applied in the workplace environment. This is submitted at the end of the placement and gives students the opportunity to discuss and reflect on key issues they have identified that relate to their placement organisation and its context. Summative assessment is provided with the end-of-module presentation where students across languages and types of activity communicate and learn from each other in so as to also foster a broad, cross cultural understanding of language-based professional and business contexts.

4.   Discussion and conclusion

The focus on reflective learning on cross cultural environments makes the module a useful preparation for the year abroad and, in due course, I hope it will inform a more nuanced understanding of what might be a recognition framework for linguistic and intercultural competence.

Very importantly, the course also establishes a mutually productive engagement between staff in a university languages department, faculty employability, central careers, the Lancaster University Students Union, and local and European companies with a language focus. We hope to strengthen these ties by building innovative and interdependent relationships that inform and stimulate research and teaching on the 'real world' contexts of Modern Languages.

To return to the faculty-wide project that kick-started this module, it is important that this module works in a supportive academic context. To enhance employability across the faculty, we have a Faculty Employability Forum whose primary focus is on information sharing on new developments in the faculty. We have had workshops to ensure robust preparation for academic reflective practice, and it is envisaged that some work on academic reflection and the different ways in which departments in the faculty embed skills into the curriculum will continue to be shared and discussed. This way, we would ensure the development of a variety of innovative assessments and to collate and build understanding of needs of, for example, professional bodies relevant to students across the many disciplines that languages work with productively.

It is also envisaged for the coming academic year that this module will be taken by visiting international students to Lancaster University. We have a new Erasmus agreement with a University Education Studies department in Spain that will provide both teacher training modules and short teaching placements for Lancaster students. In return, Spanish students will be able to take the 'Professional Contexts' module and take part in language teaching support in local schools. Given the language needs of local schools, this seems on course to be a fruitful development. It has brought the possibility of opening up the module to Erasmus students from all over Europe and integrating them in a programme of learning that can truly deliver what this course seeks: to bring together multilingual communication skills, international intercultural awareness, and business and customer awareness.

Acknowledgements

Many thanks to various staff across Lancaster University: Frank Dawes, Kate Dunbavan, Sarah Fox, Chris May and Charlotte Stuart for their collaboration on the FASS/HEA 'Embedding employability' project and their support in thinking through work-based learning. In particular, I am grateful to Frank and his invaluable work on mapping and modelling employability skills.

References and links

CBI/NUS. (2011). *Working towards your future: making the most of your time in higher education.* London: CBI. Retrieved from http://www.nus.org.uk/Global/CBI_NUS_Employability%20report_May%202011.pdf

CBI/Pearson education and skills survey. (2014). *Gateway to growth.* Retrieved from http://www.cbi.org.uk/media/2807987/gateway-to-growth.pdf

Cole, D., & Tibby, M. (2013). Defining and developing your approach to employability: a framework for higher education institutions. The Higher Education Academy.

Dawes, F., Fox, S., & Gomez-Cash, O. (2016). *Developing a flexible framework for embedding work-based modules in the curriculum.* Faculty of Arts and Social Sciences, Lancaster University. York: HEA. Retrieved from https://www.heacademy.ac.uk/resource/developing-flexible-framework-embedding-work-based-learning-modules-curriculum

Jones, H. M., & Warnock, L. (2014). Towards a competency framework for student work based learning. The Higher Education Academy.

British Academy. (2014). *Interim findings of the Born Global research project.* Retrieved from http://www.britac.ac.uk/policy/Born_Global.cfm

Section 2.

The professional linguist

10 Career adventures from learning languages

Paul Kaye[1]

1.   Personal journey in languages

Learning and using languages has been a central feature of most of my working life. In my current job, I help to promote multilingualism, language learning and the language industry in the UK, as well as to raise awareness of careers in the EU civil service for those with language knowledge. I am on temporary secondment from the European Commission's translation service, where I worked as a translator for five years. I am steeped in language talk every day, but even in earlier phases of my career, where languages were not the primary focus, knowing them has always given me an advantage and has been essential in making the next career move.

I had a monolingual British upbringing and my language journey started with just a single one: French was the only modern language that my local comprehensive offered, and it became my best and favourite subject at school. It seemed to come very naturally: I had always liked mimicking voices and accents, and speaking French just involved putting on a French accent and using French words instead of English ones. I was helped hugely by three exchange visits to France during my school years. But for a reason I still can't fathom, I thought I wanted to be a doctor and so chose sciences for A-level, dropping the French that I had loved.

My sixth form college did have a German teacher, however, and so I signed up to do an O-level in that alongside the A-levels. By the first day of term I was looking forward to the German more than the sciences, but a timetable clash meant I couldn't do the German after all. I was crestfallen, and although I have

---

1. Language Officer, European Commission Representation in the UK, London, United Kingdom; paul.kaye@ec.europa.eu

How to cite this chapter: Kaye, P. (2016). Career adventures from learning languages. In E. Corradini, K. Borthwick and A. Gallagher-Brett (Eds), *Employability for languages: a handbook* (pp. 69-72). Dublin: Research-publishing.net. http://dx.doi.org/10.14705/rpnet.2016.cbg2016.465

---

since cobbled together a knowledge of German, it is patchy and passive and I still greatly regret that language door closing on me at 16. I really wish I knew German better: it has been an important language in all the places I've worked and fluency in it would definitely have helped my career.

It was quickly clear that I wasn't doctor material, and I ended up studying biology at university. There I had an enormous stroke of luck: I managed to get onto an option to spend a year studying biology in France, with support from the EU's Erasmus programme. My A-level results wouldn't have been good enough to get me the year abroad outright, but someone dropped out of the course in the first year and I was able to replace them. The year in France gave me an experience of living abroad and the taste for learning more languages. Its presence on my CV was directly responsible for getting me my first 'serious' job and indirectly responsible for getting me the job I do now.

Before then, however, there was another language interlude: after university I wanted to see the world a little. I trained to become a teacher of English as a foreign language, and found myself teaching adults in Bratislava, the capital of Slovakia, which at that time was a new country emerging from the end of communism in Eastern Europe and the breakup of Czechoslovakia. It was a fascinating time to be there. Alongside teaching the locals my own tongue, I threw myself into learning their language, Slovak. I had no inkling of it at the time, but this urge to learn a new language also had a fundamental effect on my career path.

2. Language knowledge multiplies work opportunities

After a year of teaching, I found a job working as a journalist and broadcaster for the English-language section of the Slovak national radio station's foreign broadcasting service. I was considered for this position only because I had started to learn Slovak, and the job itself accelerated my ability in the language. Before long I was confident enough to start taking freelance translation work – and since there were virtually no other native English speakers around at that time who could read Slovak, I quickly gained a lot of clients. I also began working part-time as an in-house translator and interpreter for the Bratislava office of Deloitte, a large business services company. By the time I returned to the UK after three and a half years, I knew the language well and had a good amount of experience in translation and interpreting.

Working life then took another new turn: I had become interested in environmental issues and decided to study for a master's degree in European environment policy. But first I had to earn the money to pay for my study, and again languages came to my aid: I set up as a freelance translator of Slovak and the closely-related language of Czech. After a year's work, which included a very interesting job for Manchester United during a Champions League fixture, including interpreting for Sir Alex Ferguson in the post-match press conference, I had earned enough to start my master's degree.

The first job I was offered after the master's was as a journalist, based in London and responsible for writing about European policymaking on the environment. My new boss told me that my knowledge of French had been a major factor in giving me the job. It was also crucial in his offer of a promotion a few months later: a move to Brussels to become the news service's EU correspondent. In that role, knowing French often helped me to get ahead – particularly when reporting on decisions made by the European Court of Justice, whose judgements always appear first in French.

A few years later I was ready for another challenge and again my earlier decisions to learn languages gave me an option I wouldn't have had otherwise: I saw an advertisement for translators to work for the EU civil service. The minimum requirement is an ability to translate from two EU languages into one other. Slightly to my surprise, I passed the recruitment tests and a while later began working for the European Commission as a translator. One wonderful thing about the job has been the training we get to learn even more languages – I've been lucky to follow courses in three other European languages, and that knowledge will surely be useful to me wherever my career takes me next.

The organisation I work for, the European Union, is probably the biggest employer of linguists in the world: it has over 4,000 translators and interpreters on staff, and thousands more working on a freelance basis, all of whom serve the EU's language regime, in which all 24 official languages have equal status. This means all legislation, and many meetings, are translated and interpreted into all 24 languages. Staff linguists need to know at least two languages to be recruited, and many come to know several more over their careers. Cuts to the EU's budget have meant a reduction in staff numbers, but the EU still recruits many linguists each year and is likely to continue to do so. The volume of documents that need translating is increasing, and for translators into English in particular, the range of languages used is wide: we have a persistent deficit of native-level English speakers who are able to translate from the EU's less commonly studied languages, like Bulgarian, Estonian and Portuguese.

The advent of new translation and interpreting technologies seems not to be slowing recruitment in the sector: the EU has embraced these technologies as essential to improving its linguistic work. The use of translation memory software helps to ensure consistency of terminology across legislative texts and to accelerate the translation of repetitive documents. There is a popular conception that machine translation technologies such as Google Translate will eventually remove the need for humans to do this job. This doesn't seem to be true in our organisation: the EU has developed its own machine translation technology, adapted to the administrative and legal documents that we have to deal with. Rather than replacing humans, instead it simply helps them to be more efficient. Since almost all of our translations relate in some way to legislation, it is essential to have a pair of real human eyes checking the accuracy of translations, however good the automated output.

It's clear from all this that any decision to learn a language – whether a 'big' one or a 'small' one – is a decision that will increase career options for finding work. In my profession, as a translator and occasional interpreter, knowing another language is obviously a fundamental requirement, but the same principle holds across many different sectors of activity, however central languages are to the work being done.

11 The Professional Linguist: language skills for the real world

Mary Murata[1]

Abstract

This chapter reports on a compulsory final year employability skills module for Modern Foreign Languages (MFL) undergraduates at York St John University. The 'Professional Linguist' aims to equip students with a range of skills which they may need when entering the workplace, whilst underpinning it with theory which would benefit those wishing to continue into postgraduate study in the field. The module covers a range of skills, from IT-based ones such as use of specialist software, online dictionaries, etc., to discussion of the ethics of recent developments in translation such as fansubbing and machine translation. The module also incorporates other elements including an introduction to interpreting, using the language features in Microsoft (MS) Word and talks from professionals such as subtitlers and project managers in recognition that not all graduates will go on to become translators.

Keywords: translation, interpreting, translation theory, ethics of translation, employability skills.

1. Context and rationale

When students graduate from an MFL degree, in addition to the skills in the given language(s), they also need a range of skills which will stand them in good

---

1. York St John University, York, United Kingdom; M.Murata@yorksj.ac.uk

How to cite this chapter: Murata, M. (2016). The Professional Linguist: language skills for the real world. In E. Corradini, K. Borthwick and A. Gallagher-Brett (Eds), *Employability for languages: a handbook* (pp. 73-82). Dublin: Research-publishing.net. http://dx.doi.org/10.14705/rpnet.2016.cbg2016.466

stead when job hunting and in the workplace. Statistics show that MFL graduates are in high demand: they are the highest earners in the Arts, Creative Arts, and Humanities fields, and at least 86% of MFL graduates are in employment or further study six months after graduation, which is above the national average (Kempster, 2015). They enter a huge range of career sectors which require a wealth of skills above and beyond pure language skills.

2.   Aims and objectives

This chapter is an illustrative case study demonstrating how we embed employability skills in the curriculum, some of the challenges we have faced and how we have overcome them.

3.   What we did

This module is delivered across 12 weeks with two hours of class time per week. In weeks two to eight, one of the hours takes the form of language-specific translation tutorials in the four languages that we offer to degree level; the remaining class time is taught in a multi-language group.

3.1.   Technology for translators

The workplace for most linguists has been revolutionised by technology and is constantly evolving, so technology is central to the module. There is a general assumption that young people of the so-called 'net generation' or 'digital natives', that is to say young people who have grown up in the digital era, are universally savvy and at ease with all digital communications and technology. This assumption is not always borne out in reality, and while they may be proficient at using Facebook and eBay, many of them have poor skills in using standard workplace technologies such as MS word or using different languages or scripts on screen. The technology side of the module comprises lectures and hands-on workshops covering:

- IT skills for linguists

- Introduction to Computer Assisted Translation (CAT) tools

- Machine translation (MT) – how it works and how to use it wisely

- Subtitling

IT skills for linguists: this covers language-related skills such as how to set up a language on Windows for typing in a non-alphabetic script, advanced features of MS Word such as the review function/track changes for proofreading or collaboration, and how to use the spell check in non-English languages. These skills are reinforced over the following weeks with class activities.

CAT tools: as increasing numbers of professional translators use CAT tools, knowledge of the principles behind them and some insight into how they work is essential for people wishing to enter the profession. We use Wordfast Anywhere – a free online tool which offers many of the features of the paid-for CAT tools but is open source.

The advantage is that students can become familiar with the principles of CAT tools – translation memory, glossaries, etc., and the terminology such as source, target, fuzzy match and segment. One of the benefits of using a CAT tool can be seen when working on a document with complex formatting such as text boxes in Powerpoint. The CAT tool separates the text from the formatting for translation and then replaces the target text in the original formatting, thereby saving translators a lot of time. As an exercise, students translate a PowerPoint document and there is a great sense of satisfaction when they open their final document with exactly the same formatting but in the target language.

We supply a small glossary and translation memory file for the task, but in Wordfast Anywhere, these features can be difficult to use, as the students do not have the time to build up a translation memory for themselves and so find it difficult to see the real benefit of using a translation memory tool.

MT: all language students are familiar with MT, the most well-known being Google Translate. They often have very strong opinions on the output from Google Translate, either dismissing it as rubbish or seeing it as a godsend when they are struggling with homework. MT coupled with controlled input and post-editing is revolutionising translation, and it is currently used in a number of large multilingual institutions such as the National Assembly for Wales and the European Commission. In future, it is likely that many linguists will find employment post-editing the output of MT systems.

This remains a controversial aspect of the translation industry, but we encourage our students to make a judgement based on knowledge rather than assumptions. As well as attending a lecture on the background, history and current trends in MT, the students carry out a mini-project where they compare the output from several different internet based MT systems. This gives them an opportunity to form their own opinions on MT and learn to use it wisely. We choose free online programmes as then students can use them after graduation as well. The shortcoming of free programmes is that, unlike paid-for software, you cannot 'train' the programme by adding your own glossaries or dictionaries.

Subtitling: this is the form of translation that is most familiar to everyone, including non-linguists. It is also the form of translation which is most open to scrutiny and criticism, with both source and target text being available at the same time. Even people with minimal knowledge of a language take delight in spotting 'mistakes' in subtitles without being fully aware of the constraints that subtitlers work under. The purpose of this section of the module is to give the students an insight into the constraints of subtitling (condensing language, on screen limits on number of letters per line, number of lines, timing, etc.). We use the subtitling feature of YouTube which is freely available but offers many of the features of professional subtitling software. It is user-friendly with online tutorials available and students seem to enjoy this part of the course very much.

Student feedback to the technology-based side of the course is extremely positive; they can see the immediate benefit of familiarity with a range of technologies that have applications in the workplace. They also enjoy the practical hands-on aspect. The use of open software in the classroom means that the students become familiar with software that they can use any time after graduation – there is nothing more frustrating than being taught how to use a sophisticated piece of software that you cannot afford and have no access to later. It gives them a grounding in the terminology and features of the software types and provides an opportunity to discuss ethics and issues surrounding copyright, ownership and intellectual property.

3.2.   Translation theory and practice

This aspect of the course prepares students not only for careers using languages, but also gives them an insight into what would be involved in postgraduate courses in Translation Studies. Topics covered are:

- Translation theory and methodology

- Current trends in translation

- Introduction to interpreting

Translation theory: these lectures encourage students to reflect on the process of translation and apply this knowledge to the work set in the language-specific translation sessions. This also equips them with the metalanguage and knowledge required if they choose to take translation studies further. Often translation theory seems to be divorced from applied translation in the workplace, but our modules encourage students to apply the theory and see the relevance of it. Almost all students have had experience of translation, perhaps in school or whilst on placement in their host university. Often they have never reflected on the process, so this part of the module encourages them to reflect on and discuss their translation decisions.

Current trends: the internet provides many opportunities for amateur translation such as fansubbing, crowdsourcing, scanlation, etc and students are often familiar with the concepts, although they may not have heard the terms. Some even have experience of being on a fansubbing team for anime or games. This part of the module provides an opportunity to discuss ethical issues surrounding the increase of amateur translation such as (low) pay, loss of jobs, benefits for the fans, ethics (copyright), etc. Discussion of the issues provides not only a framework for considering their own position as future translators but lays the groundwork for the possibility of further study in the field at postgraduate level.

Interpreting: most students have some experience of informal interpreting, so in this part of the module we are able to draw on their own experiences and relate them to theory and practice. Students do a range of training activities such as shadowing, note taking, etc., to experience what would be involved in interpreter training if they took it further.

3.3.   Group project

One of the distinguishing features of the module is the group project, which is compulsory but not assessed. The students take part in a multi-lingual translation project, in which they are divided into teams comprising a project manager, translators, editors/proofreaders and (depending on the medium of the translation) subtitle time coders. The role of the project manager is to act as a hub for the project, liaising between the client (played by the lecturers) and the various members of the team. Each year the project changes dependent on overall student numbers, as well as numbers per individual language and student feedback. In previous years, the project has taken the form of translating content for a Tour de Yorkshire website, a FIFA World Cup website and similar topical themes. Most recently it took the form of a subtitling project to create multi-lingual versions of a two-minute promotional video for the University. The remit of each team was to produce a final video in each of the languages represented in their group.

The skills required for the project are:

*   Project management

- Subtitling (using free online software)

- Condensing (making the language on the screen suitable for use as subtitles)

- Translating

- Proofreading

- Netiquette

- Time management

Many of the skills required for the project, such as using track changes, use of subtitling software or the conventions for subtitling, were pre-taught in the weekly lectures; see Figure 1 for the project's flow.

Figure 1.   The flow of the project

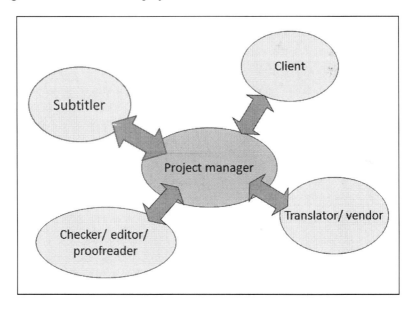

The client role is played by the lecturers. Only the project manager is allowed to communicate directly with the client. Any queries from the other team members have to go through the project manager.

The project manager is at the centre of the project, responsible for communication between the various parties and making sure the project is completed and delivered to the client on time. The project managers set deadlines and must have a contingency plan if someone lets them down.

The translator translates the English into the target foreign language; Japanese, Spanish, German or French as appropriate. Although students are mostly translating out of their strongest language, which is not standard practice, we emphasise that the purpose of the project is to experience the process and not the quality of the actual translation itself.

The subtitler copies and pastes the subtitles to the video using the software and sets the time codes as appropriate. They are required to fulfil the conventions for subtitles such as number of words on screen and length of time as taught in the subtitling theory class. The final product is delivered to the client via the project manager as a YouTube link.

We use the Virtual Learning Environment (VLE) as a project management tool replicating the kind of virtual project management tools used by many translation companies; all the files for the project are on the VLE. All communication takes place via the university email system, again replicating real world situations where the members of a team often never meet face to face. They are instructed to use language of an appropriate level of formality for a work situation and to reply promptly and politely.

As the project is not assessed, student engagement can be variable; this can be a cause of frustration for other members of the group. During the class discussion after the project, students have the opportunity to feedback to the members of their team. Often it transpires that apparent lack of engagement was due to poor time management. Each team member gives the other team members a rating out of five stars similar to the rating system on many online services such as Amazon or eBay. They rate their Likelihood of Working Again (LWA) by simply giving a number of stars in answer to the question "Would you work with this person again?" in the style of the Blue Board of the professional translation online community Proz.com. This feedback highlights the importance not only of language and practical skills but also time management, communication skills and a good work ethic.

4.   Discussion and conclusion

Student evaluation of the module is always very positive, with some students saying that it was their favourite module of the three years. A recent external examiner's report stated that it "is an excellent example of a module which aims to develop translation skills to a high level". Graduates have gone on to pursue careers in translation, interpreting, or study postgraduate translation studies.

Languages graduates can end up on a host of career paths, and they need to be equipped with skills that are transferable to a variety of workplaces. IT skills are essential in almost all jobs in the present era, so we aim to give students the skills to use a range of software, but at the same time to be reflective about their use of IT and choose wisely how and when they use the tools. The world is becoming increasingly interconnected, and yet with English apparently being the lingua franca, it is tempting to think that there is no place for translation skills in the workplace. We aim to demonstrate to our students that there is still a very important role for skilled linguists, and that judicious use of technology can enhance their skills as a linguist and boost their chances of gaining employment in a competitive world.

References and links

Kempster, H. (2015) *Arts, creative arts and Humanities overview.* Retrieved from http://www.hecsu.ac.uk/assets/assets/documents/wdgd_arts_humanities_2015.pdf

Proz.com Blue Board: http://www.proz.com/lwa?sp_mode=overview

Wordfast Anywhere: http://www.freetm.com/

12 Real language meets real business

Bill Muirhead[1] and Sarah Schechter[2]

1. Introduction

The Real Business Language Challenge was a collaborative pilot project
between Coca-Cola Enterprises (CCE) and Routes into Languages East for Year
9 and 10 pupils. It was based on CCE's award-winning Real Business Challenge,
part of its highly acclaimed education programme. The Real Business Language
Challenge transformed the project into a language and enterprise task, thus
enhancing cross-curricular opportunities (Languages with Business Studies/
PHSE/ Citizenship). It was felt that since language is a great employability
asset, supporting schools with teaching and encouraging the uptake of modern
languages fits with – and indeed, boosts – the overall objective of the programme:
to increase learners' employability and enterprise skills (in particular teamwork,
problem-solving, creative thinking, leadership, financial capability and business
acumen), giving them a competitive edge in today's job market.

Keywords: employability, enterprise, cultural awareness, cross-curricular.

2. What we did

Initially we adapted the standard Real Business Challenge model and ran a
pilot project, with the students forming teams (or small 'companies') of six
to eight to develop a healthy juice brand that took inspiration from one of the
nations competing in the next Special Olympics World Games. The students

1. Coca-Cola Entreprises Ltd, Uxbridge, United Kingdom; bmuirhead@cokecce.com

2. Routes into Languages East, Cambridge, United Kingdom; sarah.schechter@anglia.ac.uk

How to cite this chapter: Muirhead, B., & Schechter, S. (2016). Real language meets real business. In E. Corradini,
K. Borthwick and A. Gallagher-Brett (Eds), *Employability for languages: a handbook* (pp. 83-86). Dublin: Research-publishing.net. http://dx.doi.org/10.14705/rpnet.2016.cbg2016.467

had to choose a country where the target language (French, Spanish or German) was spoken. When developing their product and brand, students needed to take inspiration from the culture of a country that was competing in the Special Olympics. In particular, they were required to:

- form teams ('companies');

- create a company profile and showcase it on their PowerPoint, ensuring that they worked together as a team, sharing and delegating tasks;

- respond to the brief by carrying out market research, developing their brand (including logo design, slogan, packaging design and labelling), researching the country of origin and its culture, researching the nutritional content, completing cost and profit projection and promoting the product; and finally

- use no more than 10 slides to present their ideas on PowerPoint, giving their juice brand overview, including information on their company profile, market research, artwork, drink details, ingredients and nutritional information, brand development and packaging, cost and profit projection.

The project was supported by a comprehensive Teacher's Pack, adapted from the original version which can be found by signing up here: http://www.therealexperience.co.uk/the-real-business-challenge.

All tasks had to be completed in the target language, providing an ideal opportunity to introduce authentic, contextualised functional language in class as well as the need to explore cultural issues in class. There was flexibility in how teachers taught towards this.

The winning group, from King's Ely School, was invited to the Real Business Challenge Regional Final at Norwich City Football Club for a day of language tasks, where they were supported by a Coca-Cola Enterprises mentor who spoke and used the target foreign language (Spanish) in their role. At this event, the pupils were tasked with developing a campaign to promote awareness of the Special Olympics and presenting their campaign to a panel of experts using the foreign language.

3.   Discussion of outcomes

The pilot project was very well received and 34 teachers registered for it – in our experience a very high number for a pilot project (about 300% more than one would expect). We therefore feel that this project merits a case study, not because of its success in numbers, but perversely because of the paucity of entries and fact that that positive reception of the concept, had failed to translate into a high level of entries. We endeavoured to discover more and our investigations yielded the following qualitative responses:

"I love the concepts but am under pressure in particular this year (we have a weaker cohort)".

"It looks very interesting and motivating".

"I was hoping we could get together an entry for this but timescales were just too difficult".

"We just didn't get organised in time to run the project – we had a re-shuffle in the department (lots of teacher absence) and the groups taking part ended up switching around so I'm afraid it's fallen through".

"Not submitting this time. However, it did inspire our Business Studies Dept in concept".

"I think it is a fantastic project because it is around a topic that I think will engage young people and it includes all kinds of skills that they need to develop".

Most felt that the problems were theirs and were due to the exigencies of everyday life in a Language Department. There were very positive comments on the idea of the project itself and the potential learning outcomes. Many said that they would like to run it the following year and embed it in their Schemes of Work. A few expressed the desire for more support from Routes into Languages in running the project. This has led us to rethink the project and provide more support and scaffolding for the busy teachers.

4. Conclusion

The above journey has led us to the conclusion that the project was a valuable one and should be continued in some form, but it needs to be adapted to ensure its success, so this year we will be exploring the possibility of incorporating the project into an on-campus Language and Business Enterprise Day, working with schools to prepare the students in advance. In addition, Routes into Languages East partners at the University of East Anglia have been awarded AHRC funding to support the funding of their follow-on intercultural communication business challenge.

Reference and link

The Real Business Challenge: http://www.therealexperience.co.uk/the-real-business-challenge

13 You're the business – a custom-made business challenge for modern languages students

Jean-Christophe Penet[1]

Abstract

Modern Languages (ML) students often express concerns about their perceived lack of commercial awareness, worrying that this will put them at a disadvantage, compared with business graduates for instance, when applying for jobs. To try and change this perception, Newcastle University's School of Modern Languages (SML) teamed up with the Careers Service and two other Schools to design a custom-made, annual Business Challenge aimed at strengthening their business awareness and their confidence in their ability to thrive in a business-like environment. The challenge aims to make ML students engage with the concepts of enterprise and entrepreneurship, which can be crucial for those embarking on a career as freelance translator, for instance. It is also a way to expose students to a variety of employers, thus giving them a unique opportunity to network and to explore new avenues when applying for graduate schemes.

Keywords: business project, confidence, employability, entrepreneurship, experts, networks, soft skills.

1.   Context and rationale

Most of our modern languages students rightly believe that being fluent in languages other than English is a plus on the job market. CBI's *Education and Skills Survey 2015: Inspiring Growth* confirmed this by showing that the

---

1. Newcastle University, Newcastle upon Tyne, United Kingdom; Jean-Christophe.Penet@newcastle.ac.uk

How to cite this chapter: Penet, J.-C. (2016). You're the business – a custom-made business challenge for modern languages students. In E. Corradini, K. Borthwick and A. Gallagher-Brett (Eds), *Employability for languages: a handbook* (pp. 87-94). Dublin: Research-publishing.net. http://dx.doi.org/10.14705/rpnet.2016.cbg2016.468

---

proportion of businesses with no need for employees with language skills dropped to only 23% in 2015 compared to 35% the previous year (CBI/Pearson, 2015, pp. 41-42). Unfortunately, however, this is not the full picture. A decade ago, James Coleman made the point that despite high employment levels for language graduates six months after graduating, the proportion of modern languages students in graduate-level jobs is not always so promising (Coleman, 2004, p. 17). Many of our final-year students are aware of this difficulty and express concerns about their perceived lack of 'commercial awareness'. Rightly or wrongly, they worry that this will put them at a disadvantage compared to business graduates, for instance, when applying for graduate jobs in general and for prestigious, competitive graduate schemes in particular. Such a dichotomy can be explained, according to Canning (2009), by the fact that "languages have been largely promoted as a skill (at all levels), rather than as a humanities discipline from which students will graduate with humanities type skills such as intercultural competence, independent learning, self-motivation, etc." (p. 2). Interestingly for this case study, he then adds that this "skill/discipline rationale has interesting parallels with Mathematics, the use of which is important for a whole range of disciplines including Economics, Physical Sciences, Business, Accounting, etc., and their related professions" (Canning, 2009, p. 2). In an attempt to bridge this gap, we try at Newcastle University's SML to follow closely recommendation number eight of the Worton Review on languages by "working more proactively on skills development and careers advice and guidance" (HEFCE, 2009, p. 37).

As the School's Employability Officer, I am therefore constantly on the lookout for new initiatives that will allow our students to develop a greater awareness of all the 'other' soft skills they are developing while studying with us apart from pure linguistic skills – e.g. communication and interpersonal skills, critical reasoning, problem-solving, information-processing skills, self-awareness and motivation skills to name a few. Early 2014, I was invited by the Careers Service's Rise Up Team – a team of Entrepreneurial Development Officers tasked with helping students develop their enterprising skills – to the presentation of a university-wide simulated Business Challenge they organise every year, FLUX. The presentation aimed to make us aware of the event so we would encourage our students to take part in future events. FLUX is described by the Rise Up Team as a:

> "fast paced and fun competition which [... gets students] solving real world problems with help from business experts and top graduate employers. Working in a team of six, [students] develop, plan and present a business strategy for a real challenge that [is] unveiled at the briefing session. [They] get the chance to bounce [their] ideas off experts in key business areas before pitching [their] strategy to a Dragons' Den-style judging panel" (NU Careers Service, 2016, section 1).

FLUX is a model used by universities throughout the country and each local winning team, in addition to a GBP500 prize, gets sponsored to represent their university in the National Final.

Undeniably, participating in an event like FLUX could prove extremely advantageous to our SML students as it could help them become more aware of and make use of all their soft skills. However, FLUX in its original format potentially disadvantages SML students because they do not have formal training in business, unlike, for example, students in business-related disciplines. Adapting FLUX offered the potential to bring out soft skills and raise student awareness of the skills their language studies were giving them, and therefore, to boost their confidence. Two other schools in the Faculty of Humanities and Social Sciences (HaSS), the School of Mathematics and Statistics (Maths and Stats) and the School of Computing Science (CS) also favoured an adaptation of the FLUX model. As pointed out by Canning (2009) about maths as a subject, these two Schools have a similar skill/discipline rationale to the one we encounter in modern languages. This means that, even though their students have a very different skillset, most of them share our students' identified lack of training and experience in business. All three schools (CS, Maths and Stats, and SML) therefore decided to team up to organise a FLUX-inspired Business Challenge in a more controlled – and, therefore, reassuring – environment so our students could benefit fully from the experience.

2.   Aims and objectives

If a common objective to all three schools was to make students more confident in their soft skills by contributing to a business project through the challenge, our aims and objectives in the SML were more specifically to:

- strengthen SML students' business awareness and their confidence in their ability to thrive in a business-like environment thanks to the soft skills they have developed while studying with us;

- encourage SML students to engage with the concepts of enterprise and entrepreneurship as these can be seen as crucial for those considering self-employment (e.g. a career as freelance translator/interpreter) and demonstrating one's engagement with them can prove very useful for job interviews/selection centres;

- expose SML students to a variety of employers, thus giving them a unique opportunity to network and to explore new avenues when applying for graduate schemes.

3.   What we did

3.1.   Preparing the challenge

My colleagues from the Careers Service, CS, Maths and Stats and I met several times in Spring 2014 to discuss the timing and format of the CS, Maths and Stats and SML Business Challenge[2].

---

2. A huge thank you, here, to my colleagues Dr Phil Ansell (School of Mathematics and Statistics), Mrs Jackie Bell (Careers Service), Mr Steve Bowden (Careers Service), Ms Jos Harrison (Careers Service), Dr Dawn Weatherston (Careers Service) and Dr Steve Riddle (School of Computing Science) without whom the CS, Maths and Stats and SML Business Challenge (referred to as 'the challenge' or 'the Business Challenge' hereafter) and, therefore, this case study, could not have happened.

Concerning timing, it should be noted that the challenge is a time-consuming event as it takes place over two days; students are required to attend a briefing session on the evening of the first day (when the scenario is set) as well as the event itself the following afternoon and evening. We all agreed that the Business Challenge should take place halfway through the first semester of the academic year 2014-15. This was to ensure that participating final-year and MA students could draw on this experience when writing up their CVs and at job interviews, as quite a few major graduate schemes have a December or January application deadline.

Once suitable dates were identified, we had to decide whether the Business Challenge would be self-contained or feed into the University's annual FLUX event. We decided that our Business Challenge should be self-contained but we agreed that we would actively encourage the winning team to consider taking part in the University's FLUX event.

As the challenge must answer a real business need, we looked for a major employer that would appeal to all our students to set it. As a major employer of languages, maths and computing students, intelligence agency Government Communication Headquarters (GCHQ) was the ideal employer to set the challenge and we were very grateful they accepted to do so and send experts to help students on the day. Each school collaborated with them on the elaboration of a scenario that worked for all three schools. We then invited two other employers to act as business experts and judges on the day of the event. The SML invited two language graduates working as an established freelance translator/ interpreter and a project manager respectively, and other invited employers represented Aldi, Ernst and Young, Procter and Gamble, Santander and Teach First. All employers were carefully briefed on their role as experts and judges ahead of the event.

Finally, we agreed that each School would invite 30 students and that all 15 teams would be made up of two CS, two Maths and Stats and two SML students. We felt that having students work collaboratively with peers from other subject areas would reflect the true nature of work in a business-like environment.

3.2. The Business Challenge

The Business Challenge took place on Tuesday 18th November 2014 (5.30-7.30pm) and Wednesday 19th November (1pm-8.30pm). Participating students had to register ahead of the event. Upon arrival at the briefing session on the Tuesday evening, students were welcomed and split into teams. The scenario was then unveiled by GCHQ – students were asked to develop a business proposal on online security. They were given the rest of the session to start generating ideas and were encouraged to take part of the evening and the following morning to continue doing so.

On the next day, students were welcomed back and introduced to Alexander Osterwalder's Business Model Canvas[3] to help them develop their business idea along the following lines: key partnerships, activities and resources, value proposition of proposal and target customers, customer relationships and communication channels with customers, and, last but not least, cost structures and revenue streams. They were given three hours to do so in their teams with the help of employers and members of the Rise Up Team in their capacity as business experts. Students were also encouraged to recognise that employers were experts in different business areas and to make use of all the expertise they needed for their project, thus encouraging them to network to enhance their business proposal. All teams were then given one hour to prepare for the pitches that took place from 5-6.30pm. The teams were split into three streams of five teams and all were given ten minutes to pitch their business proposal followed by five minutes' questions in front of a panel made up of one member of GCHQ, one member of the Rise Up Team and one academic. Stream winners were then announced to the whole group and participants were given feedback on presentations. This was followed by a final, one-minute 'elevator pitch' in front of the whole group who then voted for the winning team. After some more feedback from employers and prize-giving, all students and staff were invited to a drinks reception so as to give everyone a final opportunity for networking.

---

3. http://www.businessmodelgeneration.com/canvas/bmc

4.   Discussion and conclusion

Students' feedback on the event was extremely positive with 98% of respondents very satisfied or satisfied with it. Students said the challenge helped them improve their teamwork skills, organisational skills as well as their communication and presentation skills in a 'non-intimidating environment'. An SML student said this was "one of the best things [they] have done at University – and it will be great to talk about at forthcoming interviews". Another one of our SML students emailed us to say "how fantastic I thought the Business Challenge was […], it's something that I never thought would be possible for a language student such as myself to achieve and I'm really grateful that we were given this opportunity". Such qualitative feedback from language students seems to show that we have achieved our first objective of growing our students' confidence in their ability to thrive in a business-like environment. Indeed, all employers praised students' innovative ideas and the expert from Procter and Gamble added that "it was an excellent advert of the talent in the Maths, Computing and Languages courses". Similarly, the expert from GCHQ said he hoped "some of [your students] will think of us when they come to apply for jobs". More disappointingly, a language student commented that "the scenario should be set to get Modern Languages Students more involved". Even though the scenario did not contain any language-specific elements, the task did require excellent communication skills from the teams as they had to pitch sometimes complex, technical online security processes to a lay audience. The more successful pitches were the ones that used language students to do so by letting them 'decode' the key technical message and 'encode' it back into lay language (what would be known as 'code-switching' in the language class). The feedback made us realise that we could make even more of an effort during the challenge to help our languages students realise that they do, in fact, possess the soft skills necessary for the task besides their language skills.

In December 2015, we organised a second CS, Maths and Stats and SML Business Challenge that built on the success of the first one while taking account of the more negative feedback. We followed the same format but made sure the challenge set by GCHQ took into consideration the particular strengths of languages students, for example in communication. We also made students aware of their soft skills during the briefing and insisted on the importance of communication skills for the pitches. The second event was as successful as the first one with all respondents (80% of attendants) saying they were either very satisfied or satisfied with the event and that it "increased their understanding of how to develop a business idea". The qualitative feedback was equally positive with one student saying "I feel like I've got valuable experience to add to my CV". GCHQ were so impressed with the quality of the business proposals put forward by finalists that they invited them to present their ideas at a meeting of Newcastle Chapter of Open Web Application Security Project (OWASP) that gathers employers from across the region in January 2016. Boosted by this incredible outcome we intend to organise a third Business Challenge next year that may include students from another school, the School of Psychology. I hope that colleagues will see from this case study that this formula for a custom-made Business Challenge, which can easily be replicated elsewhere, can help our language students become aware of all the soft skills they have gained through their studies with us. This should also make them confident that, when it comes to business, they have a huge amount of skills to offer!

References and links

Canning, J. (2009). A skill or a discipline? An examination of employability and the study of modern foreign languages. *Journal of Employability and the Humanities, 3*, 1-12. Retrieved from http://eprints.soton.ac.uk/50392/1/JCanningArticle.pdf

CBI/Pearson. (2015). Education and skills survey 2015: inspiring growth. Retrieved from http://news.cbi.org.uk/reports/education-and-skills-survey-2015/

Coleman, J. (2004). Languages and careers. In J. Coleman & J. Klapper (Eds.), *Effective learning and teaching in modern languages* (pp.17-22). London: Routledge.

HEFCE. (2009). *Review of modern foreign languages provision in higher education in England* (Chairman: Professor Michael Worton). London: Higher Education Funding Council for England. Retrieved from www.ucl.ac.uk/vice-provost/worton/myimages1/worton_report.pdf

NU Careers Service. (2016). *Rise Up FLUX*. Retrieved from http://www.ncl.ac.uk/careers/riseup/skills/flux/#what

14 Plan your future! Career management skills for students of languages

Laurence Randall[1]

Abstract

At the University of Westminster, the Department of Modern Languages and Cultures has developed a student employability and work-integrated learning project, 'Career Management Skills' (CMS), for undergraduate language students. The main objective was to develop a comprehensive employability strategy for all students on all undergraduate language courses at the university. The programme has evolved to include among the employability provisions a Work Placement module, which started in the academic year 2014-2015. This case study will present the context in which both CMS and the work placement module were implemented, offer an evaluation of both, and assess their impact on students and on the undergraduate programme as a whole.

Keywords: career management skills, work placement module, student employability, undergraduate language courses.

1.   Context and rationale

For a number of years, languages departments at British universities have had to be restructured, or in several cases closed, because of the predominance of the English language in the job market and the government's non-prioritisation of foreign languages for secondary schools. However, the University of Westminster's Department of Modern Languages and Cultures (MLC) is

1. University of Westminster, London, United Kingdom; L.L.Randall@westminster.ac.uk

How to cite this chapter: Randall, L. (2016). Plan your future! Career management skills for students of languages. In E. Corradini, K. Borthwick and A. Gallagher-Brett (Eds), *Employability for languages: a handbook* (pp. 95-102). Dublin: Research-publishing.net. http://dx.doi.org/10.14705/rpnet.2016.cbg2016.469

relatively healthy, with 504 undergraduate and postgraduate students in 2015, despite the closure of German in 2014. Paradoxically, it is the job market itself (or to employ the buzzword, 'employability') that seems to help the MLC to hold its ground, as with globalisation, job prospects for humanities graduates increase if students can demonstrate that they can speak a foreign language (Tinsley & Board, 2013, pp. 6, 12, 24; Beyene, 2012). Employability has in turn generated new initiatives that have made language degree courses more attractive to school-leavers.

Hence, in 2008 the University of Westminster's Centre of Excellence for Professional Learning in the Workplace (now Westminster Exchange) funded a student employability and work-integrated learning project to be developed in the Department of Modern and Applied Languages entitled CMS, designed for undergraduate language students at all levels. An Employability Coordinator post was created and I was appointed to develop the project.

2.   Aims and objectives

At the genesis of the CMS project and before implementation, we had three objectives:

- Develop a comprehensive employability strategy for all students enrolled on all undergraduate language courses at the university.

- Maximise student, staff and employer engagement in, and awareness of, the real-world applications of language skills and cultural knowledge.

- Challenge perceptions about the boundaries that separate work from learning in the broad disciplinary area of languages (Robertson, n.d, p. 1).

Employers often view language skills as peripheral to the core attributes they seek, and some students can adopt the same perception. It was therefore seen as imperative to enable students to bridge that perceptual gap. The next step was to develop workshops that would be embedded in the curriculum, which would allow language students to enhance their employment-related competencies.

3.   What we did

3.1.   The embedding of CMS

In order to understand how CMS was embedded in the curriculum, it is vital to appreciate the main components of the Undergraduate Language Curriculum at the University of Westminster. Apart from BA French Translation or BA Spanish Translation, all degrees are joint degrees combining languages with another discipline: English Language, English Literature, Linguistics, or International Relations. The Languages Undergraduate programme has three strands articulated around four languages (Arabic, Chinese, French and Spanish):

- First, the core curriculum year-long Language Development module (30 credits). Language is developed both as an object of study and as a means of increasing cultural awareness – part of the four elements identified in the 'Languages and Related Studies' benchmark statements (QAA, 2007). Training is provided in the four key language skills (reading, speaking, listening and writing) with a focus on culture.

- Second, the semester-long Area Studies module (15 credits). It focuses on languages as a means of developing cultural awareness and enables students to develop research skills and intercultural competence through documents in English and in the target language.

- Third, the semester-long 'Languages in Action' module (15 credits). This strand uses languages as a means of communication in real-life scenarios which, depending on the student's level of language, will lead up to work-related settings.

As in 'Languages in Action', students use their language and graduate skills within professional contexts, and in order to help students to develop their Professional Development Plan, it was in this particular strand that CMS was embedded at all levels of studies as an hour-long workshop in each semester.

The CMS workshops are not an add-on but an integrated component of the module, embedded incrementally across all three years of the course in the Learning Aims and Outcomes of the Languages in Action strand. All the elements in this strand were approved by external examiners as part of the course validation and revalidation.

At the workshops, students learn how to articulate and present their skills and competencies, enhancing their employability.

3.2. Content of the CMS workshops

Designing the CMS workshop entailed drawing up a specific programme at each level of study and for each semester; (1) designing PowerPoint presentations, practical exercises, reflective log sheets, and an e-portfolio, and (2) constructing a Blackboard site where students could locate all materials. I engaged the expertise of the Career Development Centre and Blackboard team whose help was invaluable in building the PowerPoint presentations and configuring the Blackboard site. The University of Westminster purchased the use of a professional website, 'My Career', created by the University of Reading[2]. The CMS Blackboard site has direct links to 'My Career' tailored to the content of the workshops. Initially, the content of the workshops was as follows:

- **First year**: Semester 1: Self-awareness; Semester 2: Covering letters and CVs.

- **Second year**: Semester 1: Opportunity awareness; Semester 2: Application forms.

---

2. Students access 'My Career' by registering on our online Engage platform: https://engage.westminster.ac.uk/students/abintegro/

- **Third year**: Semester 1: Assessment Centres; Semester 2: Interviews.

A team of three CMS lecturers was trained by the Career Development Centre to deliver these workshops. Regular feedback from students and CMS lecturers revealed that some adjustments to the workshops were needed. For example, Level 6 students felt that the Semester 1 workshop on assessment centres was too daunting and not necessarily appropriate to the kind of employment and companies they would seek in the near future; they requested a more practical workshop. Accordingly, I selected and invited employers from a variety of sectors to deliver workshops on 'Job opportunities for Language Students', targeted to the students' language skills to help students revisit their positioning on the job market. However, some students felt that some of the employer presentations were not particularly relevant to the kind of employment they wished to pursue, leading to further modifications of this particular workshop. The Level 5, Semester 1 workshops also needed some adjustments; students wanted to target their application form to internships and the workshop was slightly altered to reflect this.

The CMS venture met with a degree of resistance from lecturers and students. Some lecturers felt that the injection of employability in their module was superfluous and was taking one hour per semester away from the teaching of the language, since they felt that they 'owned' the dedicated weekly two-hour slot. This in turn was reflected in the perception of the non-usefulness of the CMS workshops by some students. Additionally, as CMS is not credit-bearing and does not count towards the overall degree mark, some students felt they did not have to do the coursework, as for them non-credit-bearing meant non-compulsory. Also, a small number of mature students who had their career fully mapped out felt that they had little to learn from CMS.

To restore students' appreciation of the connection between employability and university studies, I was able to secure sponsorship from two businessmen keen to support our students in their career planning. We were able to award three prizes per semester at each level for the best Reflective Logs submitted on time at the School Registry Office: the first prize was GBP150, the second prize GBP100 and the third prize GBP50. The CMS prizes and award certificates were handed out at a special CMS award ceremony conducted by the Head of Department. On the whole, most students engaged in this form of reflective practice and showed a real need and thirst to articulate the skills acquired during their studies.

3.3.   Internships

As mentioned by Robertson (n.d), the CMS project exploits "the range and diversity of language-related employment and voluntary opportunities that central London offers" (p. 1). Internships have been developed both in Britain and abroad. Internships abroad come from a variety of employment sectors: town halls, university, estate agents, conference centres, tourist offices, and primary and secondary schools. Students engaged in various tasks ranging from website translation to property valuation, reception work, and teaching. Internships in Britain encompass a variety of sectors: museums, showrooms and galleries, energy-saving companies, the hospitality sector, sports, and media.

3.4.   Work placement module

For annual monitoring, I conducted a focus group on the employability provisions in MLC with a sample of students from each year-group. Feedback revealed that students would favour a graded employability programme that included a work placement module. This report was submitted to the MLC Head of Department who supported the idea and facilitated the transition. We kept the CMS workshops at Level 4 and I designed a module *pro forma* for a new work placement module which would be offered to students during the second year and third year of their studies. We were actually the only department in the Faculty not offering a work placement module among option modules.

The work placement module/work shadowing experience in a language/culture setting is a year-long module bearing 15 credits. It provides students with the opportunity to work for a minimum of 30 hours in a setting related to their studies. The aim is to develop professional skills, and apply language skills/ cultural knowledge in a real-world work situation. The placement is chosen and organised by students, but must be validated by the module leader. However, I have been actively engaged in finding relevant employer contacts to facilitate students' approach to employers in order to secure a work placement. Students who have worked during the summer can also ask for validation of this work placement as part of their module. The work placement module is intended to be primarily experiential. Students are required to attend four two-hour workshops during the course of the module, focusing on networking skills, researching a company, identifying and developing transferable skills and writing a 1000-word reflective statement based on a diary kept during the work placement, and a 2500-word report on a salient area of the organisation. Anticipating that the module would be popular, course leaders asked for the module to be capped at 30 students so as not to imperil other option modules whose content is more language-based. Indeed, the module, which has now been running for two years, has proved very popular. Registration is on a first-come-first-served basis and there is always a waiting-list. However, the work placement module attracts two types of students: those who are really interested in acquiring work experience, and those who perceive it as an 'easy module' due to the limited number of workshops to attend. Students have demonstrated varying degrees of engagement in securing placements, and in the first year there were some anxieties regarding the two pieces of coursework, which led in the second year to tutorials being offered to support students in writing their coursework. Nevertheless, in the module's first year of running, half the students obtained a First mark for their two pieces of coursework, and most of the remaining students achieved Upper-Second marks. The need emerged to appoint a work placement officer who would be able to oversee all placement provisions in the faculty. Our next step is to audit all the work placements and make sure they conform to Chapter B10 of the Quality Assurance Agency's Quality Code, 'Managing Higher Education provision with others'.

4.   Discussion and conclusion

All universities in Britain are undertaking a major change programme referred to as 'Learning Futures'. It started in 2012/13, aiming to introduce a revised curriculum in September 2016. The goal is to produce a simplified curriculum framework with greater course coherence, reduced assessments and more opportunities for work placements[3]. Therefore, with the implementation of the new 'Learning Futures' scheme, the whole MLC programme is being restructured with fewer modules bearing more credits. Hence, the three existing strands have been replaced with two new core semester-long modules at Level 4, worth 20 credits. There are a number of new option modules with an emphasis on culture (all worth 20 credits). The work placement module will now be in the second year only, since in their final year students need to concentrate on their exams rather than looking for work placements. Following course validation and student feedback, we have increased the number of workshops in the work placement module. There will be one workshop on modern technology as a research tool, as well as support workshops on writing the two assessment pieces. Although the cap of 30 students has been removed under the new curriculum, the work placement module will now compete with four other option modules. CMS has been removed from the curriculum mainly for budget reasons. It remains to be seen what fruit this smaller but more targeted focus on employability will produce.

References and links

Beyene, S. (2012, July 19). Language skills: way to get a job? *Guardian*. Retrieved from http://www.theguardian.com/education/2012/jul/19/optional-language-modules-degree

QAA (Quality Assurance Agency). (2007). *Languages and related studies*. Mansfield: The Quality Assurance Agency for Higher Education. Retrieved from http://www.qaa.ac.uk/en/Publications/Documents/Subject-benchmark-statement-Languages-and-related-studies.pdf

Robertson, P. (n.d). *Project brief.* Retrieved from https://www.llas.ac.uk/resourcedownloads/2912/Robertson_Multilingua_Project_Brief.doc

Tinsley, T., & Board, K. (2013). *Languages for the future: which languages the UK needs most and why*. London: British Council. Retrieved from https://www.britishcouncil.org/sites/default/files/languages-for-the-future-report.pdf

---

3. https://myintranet.westminster.ac.uk/learning-and-teaching/learning-futures

15 Communicating and teaching languages: a module for life

René Koglbauer[1], Elizabeth Andersen[2], and Sophie Stewart[3]

Abstract

This case study introduces a final year undergraduate module in the School of Modern Languages at Newcastle University. The module offers a model for embedding careers in modern languages teaching into the curriculum, and thereby enhancing student employability. The case study gives an insight into the various strands of activity undertaken by the students/ Language Ambassadors on the module. These include university-led input that focuses on the areas of language policy, pedagogy, professionalism and reflection, and a 60-hour in-school placement which allows the Language Ambassadors to gain first-hand experience of what the teaching profession is like. Through the academic assessments (a reflective report in the target language, a portfolio and a reflective essay) the academic and school experience are brought together. The authors make the argument that the module addresses the development of transferable skills that employers are looking for in employees.

Keywords: language ambassador, role model, in-school experience, reflective practitioner, professionalism, transferable skills.

1. Newcastle University, Newcastle, United Kingdom; rene.koglbauer@newcastle.ac.uk

2. Routes into Languages North East, Newcastle, United Kingdom; elizabeth.andersen@newcastle.ac.uk

3. Routes into Languages North East, Newcastle, United Kingdom; sophie.stewart2@newcastle.ac.uk

How to cite this chapter: Koglbauer, R., Andersen, E., & Stewart, S. (2016). Communicating and teaching languages: a module for life. In E. Corradini, K. Borthwick and A. Gallagher-Brett (Eds), *Employability for languages: a handbook* (pp. 103-111). Dublin: Research-publishing.net. http://dx.doi.org/10.14705/rpnet.2016.cbg2016.470

1. Context and rationale

"Communicating and Teaching Languages for Undergraduate Language Ambassadors" is an undergraduate module for final year students in the School of Modern Languages at Newcastle University. This 20 credit module, running over two semesters, was established between 2010 and 2012.

The module is aligned with the university's Career Development Module[4], where placement requirements are concerned. However, during the development phase, the decision was made that students taking this module should additionally explore various concepts of language pedagogy, language learning and teaching. From the outset it was agreed that a minimum of 30% of the final assessment should be undertaken in French, German or Spanish. The choice of languages is directly linked to the curriculum offer in placement schools in the North East. The module has been developed and delivered by linguists from the School of Modern Languages and educationalists with experience in (initial) teacher training from the School of Education, Communication and Language Sciences, emphasising not only the pedagogical aspect of this module but also the importance of being trained to reflect appropriately on the experience both in school and at university.

2. Aims and objectives

The module gives the students a grounding in the factors that have shaped language policy nationally during the last two decades. It provides an opportunity for students to observe and gain experience of teaching languages in a real classroom environment at one of the local placement schools. The partnership between the two university departments and local schools aims to foster and stimulate pupil uptake of languages beyond Key Stage. An additional aim is for final year students to be able to make an informed decision when considering teaching languages as a future career.

---

4. http://www.ncl.ac.uk/careers/develop/cdm/index.php

---

3.   What we did

The two-semester module has three equally important elements; university-based lectures and seminars, the in-school experience through a 60-hour placement, as well as the language development in at least one Modern Foreign Language (MFL). The last component was of particular importance at the development and approval stage of this module. The 30% component of assessing the students' language skills together with the active use of their target language during the school placement and in practical seminars contributed to the successful approval of this module by the School of Modern Languages for the final year curriculum offer.

The academic year commences with a joint twilight session attended by students and their mentors (MFL teachers in the placement schools). During this meeting the foci of the module are shared and students and mentors are given the opportunity to get to know each other, exchange important pieces of information both in terms of the students' ability and availability for placement visits as well as the school's/language department's priorities. As most of the mentors have been part of the module from its beginnings, students gain an initial insight into what activities they will be expected to undertake during the course of their placement.

The academic provision is delivered front-loaded, i.e. most of the university seminars take place in the first three months of the module. This is to ensure that the students have an increasing understanding in the following four overarching themes: language policy and language study in the UK, exploring the importance of reflection for the role of Language Ambassadors by developing into a reflective practitioner, language pedagogy, and professionalism in the workplace. The academic sessions are a combination of academic/research-informed input and discussions coupled with practical activities that are often student-led. Early on in the academic curriculum, the students are trained in the power of impartial observation and reflection, in particular through the Gibbs' (1988) Reflective Cycle, a tool which helps the students to articulate and structure reflections on their practical experience, both verbally and in writing.

As part of the student-led activities, students have to engage in micro-teaching episodes, preparing in pairs a ten-minute teaching sequence that they then deliver to the class. The students are asked to reflect on their experience immediately after they have delivered their sequence and receive peer-feedback from their fellow students who have acted as participant observers. Each micro-teaching pair is then given an opportunity to engage in a reflective dialogue about their performance with one of the module tutors. It is not the actual quality of the teaching episode but rather the quality of the reflection on the experience and the feedback received that counts towards the final assessment.

The final grade is an amalgamation of three assessed components: a reflective report on the use of the target language in the classroom (30%, written in the target language, submitted in semester 1), a portfolio (increased to 20% in academic year 2015-16, submitted after Easter) and an essay (reduced to 50% in 2015-16, written in English, submitted during the assessment weeks of semester 2). For the reflective report in the target language and the final essay, students use the Gibbs' (1988) cycle to structure their work.

The reflective report has as its focus the use of target language in the classroom. Students select an observed lesson and reflect on the use of target language by referring to discussions with school mentors, school policies on target language, and peer-reviewed literature. In the final essay, students are allowed to choose an aspect of language methodology and reflect upon this using an observed or self-taught session; they also have the opportunity to write a more discursive essay on the topic of language policy. Regardless of which focus they choose, students have to embed peer-reviewed literature, experience and evidence from interviews, conversations, and students' questionnaires into their writing.

The portfolio, to which a number of amendments have been made in light of students' and school mentors' feedback, consists of five tasks: an observation task, a reflection on micro-teaching, a reflection on a presentation about the importance of languages for a particular target audience (specified year groups, parents) delivered by the students themselves, a report of an interview with the headteacher/deputy head in charge of curriculum about the position of languages in the placement school, and a reflective commentary on a videoed sequence taught in the placement school.

The portfolio is the academic link between the university seminars and the school placement. Apart from the required portfolio tasks, the students and school mentors are given the freedom to design the timetable and the activities according to learners' and schools' needs and match those with the Language Ambassadors' skillset and identified areas for development. Some students will work across all year groups, some will predominantly work with exam classes; in a few instances, students work with 6th formers on developing their exam oral topics. Students have set up their own language clubs (sometimes even in their second or third language that is not a curriculum subject in the school) or contributed to open evening events for parents and prospective students, utilising the facts and presentation skills developed and enhanced through one of the portfolio tasks.

Students' feedback indicates that their performance in school should be counted towards their final academic grade. The module leaders took the conscious decision to not assess the in-school experience through formal observations as this would mean additional pressure for all parties involved (students, school mentors and their teams, and academic staff) and a less developmental approach to the experiences collated during the placement. The importance of the in-school experience and the enthusiasm, quality of reflection and active engagement in the placement school are celebrated in the portfolio submission. At the end of the academic year, each school mentor writes a brief report on each of their Language Ambassadors.

The official end of the module is marked by a twilight celebration seminar to which school mentors and Language Ambassadors are invited. During this session, the students, module tutors and school mentors reflect on the various aspects of the programme and constructive feedback is exchanged. The latter is essential to inform future developments of the academic programme but also gives school mentors an opportunity to share good practice on how to deploy Language Ambassadors.

The module requires a high level of support by an administrator (this could be additional allocation of time for one of the module tutors). The administrator is the first port of contact for school mentors and students regarding all administrative aspects: finding suitable placement schools, allocating the Language Ambassadors to their placement schools, timetable clashes, monitoring attendance of school placements, arranging school mentors' meetings, administering the expenses claims for Language Ambassadors' travel to placement schools and most importantly, ensuring that all Language Ambassadors have successfully undergone a Disclosure and Barring Service (DBS) check.

4.   Discussion and conclusion

In November 2015, the Minister of State for Universities and Science stated in his foreword to the Green Paper on Higher Education, entitled *Fulfilling Our Potential: Teaching Excellence, Social Mobility and Student Choice*, that the government will "provide greater focus on employability" (BIS, 2015, p. 8). Employability and skills development are two overarching aims of the Language Ambassador module. In the Green Paper, no reference is made to the employability of graduates from disciplines in social sciences and humanities. This might not come as a surprise, considering that the Confederation of British Industry (CBI) highlighted in their 2015 report that 40% of the surveyed employers were looking for STEM graduates, 19% for Business graduates, 5% for graduates from Social Sciences disciplines and 1% for Languages and Arts graduates (CBI, 2015, pp. 57-58). However, the CBI report states clearly the importance of language skills; 45% of employers "see foreign language ability as beneficial to the businesses" (CBI, 2015, p. 41). Over a quarter of the responding businesses reported that language skills contribute to staff mobility.

As linguists and educationalists, we have argued for decades that studying a language does not end with being fluent in a foreign language. Being able to communicate in a foreign language opens one's horizon, allows the speaker to see the world in a different light – through different cultural lenses. Studying a language requires one to be resilient and a certain degree of self-management is needed too in order to succeed. It is therefore worth analysing the CBI report further, as it reports on employers' satisfaction rates with graduates' work-relevant skills (CBI, 2015, p. 58). Figure 1 summarises some of the findings relevant for our discussion here.

Figure 1.   Percentage of employers not satisfied with stated skills (information taken from CBI, 2015, p. 58, Exhibit 80)

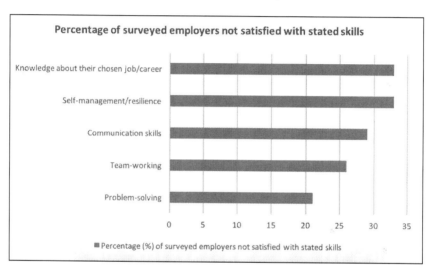

As previously stated, one of the aims of the module is to give Language Ambassadors an insight into what teaching as a profession is like; although a number of Language Ambassadors entered the teaching profession, the module is not intended to 'sell' language teaching as a profession. Module leaders and school mentors agreed from the outset that it is important for the Language Ambassadors to gain a realistic picture of teaching as a career with its many highlights, challenges, stressful moments and downs. One of our former students (academic year 2012-13) highlighted in her module feedback that "doing the module truly gave me food for thought in choosing my professional career". A fellow student (academic year 2012-13, currently enrolled in a teacher training programme) summarised his experience as follows: "The module gave me a good idea what it would be like to go into teaching". The in-school experience, the relationship that the Language Ambassadors build over the academic year with their school mentors, as well as the pupils contributes to the success story; another student (academic year 2013-14) enjoyed her placement so much that she decided to follow the School Direct route and successfully applied to her placement school; her latest message to the tutor team said "I am absolutely loving it".

Passion, resilience and self-management are key features of the module. The more passion a Language Ambassador brings to the module, and most importantly to the in-school experience and the work with the pupils, the more they will benefit and learn from it. The students experience this module as challenging and definitely more time consuming than any other 20-credit module they enrol in. Students are required to be extremely independent throughout the module; independence and self-management are necessary for the successful completion of their academic work, for the construction of their timetable, for the preparation of teaching sequences, or the organisation of the interview with the headteacher for their portfolio task. These skills, together with good communication skills, are essential for building a professional relationship with their mentors and the tutors. The academic programme is designed so that all relevant skills are discussed and explored as part of the initial university-based input. During seminar activities and portfolio tasks and through peer/tutor feedback, students will have reflected on their skill set critically, and the reflection tools with which they have been equipped will help them to identify their strengths and areas for development during the placement.

The remaining two skills which were identified as important by employers, team-working and problem-solving, are fully embedded throughout the module and are essential on the Language Ambassadors' journey to becoming a reflective participant, observer, and practitioner.

Those students who have not chosen to go into teaching after their experience have reported back that many of the acquired skills, in particular the ability to reflect on their in-school experience in response to competency questions during job interviews, has significantly helped them to secure good employment. Some Language Ambassadors do find their real passion; as one ambassador (academic year 2013-14) describes, "I never wanted to be a teacher until fourth year and I would have to say that the Language Ambassador module definitely contributed to my decision to apply to teacher training. I absolutely love my job and couldn't imagine doing anything else".

References and links

BIS. (2015). *Fulfilling our potential: teaching and excellence, social mobility and student choice. November 2015.* London: Department for Business Innovation & Skills. Retrieved from https://www.timeshighereducation.com/sites/default/files/breaking_news_files/green_paper.pdf

CBI. (2015). *Inspiring growth. CBI/Pearson Education and Skills Survey 2015.* London: CBI. Retrieved from http://news.cbi.org.uk/business-issues/education-and-skills/gateway-to-growth-cbi-pearson-education-and-skills-survey-2015/

Gibbs, G. (1988). *Learning by doing: a guide to teaching and learning methods.* London, Oxford: Further Education Unit, Oxford Brookes University.

16 Get that job! A project on the German job application process

Hanna Magedera-Hofhansl[1]

1.   Introduction

With decreasing numbers of students studying German at Higher Education Institutions in the United Kingdom, there is an increasing demand for graduate Germanists. This project, designed for C1/C2 level students according to the Common European Framework of Reference for languages, prepares finalist students for a job market in which UK and German businesses need culturally aware and competent speakers of English and German.

Through a holistic approach including reading, writing, listening and speaking, the exercises described below will increase students' professional employability skills.

Keywords: employability skills, job interview, German CV and cover letter, LinkedIn, social media profile.

2.   What I did

In the first instance, students are invited to reflect upon the specific skills that make each individual unique. We discuss the nature of 'hard skills', such as their A-levels, a university degree and language skills. As a next step we discuss 'soft skills', which comprise communication skills, the ability to work in a team or leadership experience. Students reflect upon their own 'hard skills' and 'soft skills' and give examples of how they have acquired and used them previously.

---

1. University of Liverpool, Liverpool, United Kingdom; hofhansl@liverpool.ac.uk

How to cite this chapter: Magedera-Hofhansl, H. (2016). Get that job! A project on the German job application process. In E. Corradini, K. Borthwick and A. Gallagher-Brett (Eds), *Employability for languages: a handbook* (pp. 113-116). Dublin: Research-publishing.net. http://dx.doi.org/10.14705/rpnet.2016.cbg2016.471

This could be, for example, their communication skills as student ambassadors, team leading skills by involvement in a local youth organisation or as a sports coach, or resilience when they coped well with stress successfully in a previous job. Students think about 'hard' and 'soft skills' and how they will use them in the job they are applying for, and also what they understand by transferable skills such as translation, presentation and IT. Thinking about skills enriches both undergraduates' vocabulary and their self-awareness.

As a warm-up, learners analyse a German sample *curriculum vitae* and cover letter in a reading comprehension, noting phrases and technical terms they can use, but also the format and the layout. For more advanced reading texts, learners have to research online newspapers in the target language and read tips on the application process and take these tips into account.

As a writing exercise, students are then required to write their own CV and cover letter in the target language in response to a job advertisement that they find on the website praktikum.de using the European europass website. This web-based platform offers layouts for CVs in all European languages. CVs from this platform are very well regarded in German speaking countries. Users create a *europass* user profile and log on every time they make changes. This allows users to update their CV easily, accurately and professionally and create it in several languages if needed. Furthermore, *europass* offers helpful documents relating to CV drafting that can also help in creating a professional and appealing profile on LinkedIn, the frequently used tool for networking between alumni and for various job offers within a network.

In class, students next learn about cultural differences and awareness by discussing how photos are used in German job applications. Everybody reads the article "Die Gunst des kantigen Kinns" by Andreas Ross (2003) in the *Spiegel online* magazine. The class first analyses sample photos and briefly gives reasons orally and subsequently in three to four written sentences as to why one picture might be suitable whereas another might not be. They consider the background of the images, what candidates are wearing, their facial expressions, as well as the quality of the picture, e.g. a high resolution versus a blurry picture.

Students can show their own profile photos and discuss how to make the best impression on a potential employer and whether that image would be suitable for their LinkedIn profile.

As a substantive academic written task, students write an essay of 300-350 words discussing whether photos should be used in applications, or which professions need photos in their applications, like fashion models. Whereas adding a picture to an application is not typical in the UK, online networking tools are increasingly screened by potential employers. Awareness of this can be used when preparing social media profiles for graduate job hunting. Undergraduates should be aware what images of them are available online and which could work in their favour – or not – during an application process.

A sample job interview from the online magazine Tomorrow Focus is shown and serves as the basis for a listening comprehension exercise. This gives examples of both unsuccessful and successful job interviews with an analysis by professional coaches.

In the next step, students get a list of sample questions used in job interviews which they prepare in their own time. In another lesson, they conduct mock job interviews with their language tutor taking the role of the interviewer to enhance their awareness of themselves and for speaking practice. Alternatively, as a more informal and fun speaking implementation, the language tutor distributes role cards including useful phrases typically used by interviewees and a panel of interviewers. This allows the tutor to assign the roles of moderator, interviewer, and project manager, with students using new phrases to moderate a debate.

3. Discussion of outcomes and conclusion

The elements in teaching units can be delivered over several weeks and built up until students feel well prepared and competent in tackling any job application. The outcomes of this project are linguistic, using several language skills, but they are also cultural as they foreground differences in the German and UK application process. They are also employability related because they actually practise the job interview itself in a foreign language. Job interviews are always nerve wracking, but practising them gives students the edge to perform well in a real job interview. As a follow-up exercise, a mock assessment centre situation can be set up. This final exercise provides future graduates not only with excellent and useful skills for the job market, but also an interactive role play that demands high-quality and linguistically challenging preparation and activities.

References and links

Europass: https://europass.cedefop.europa.eu/de/home

Praktikum.de: http://www.praktikum.de

Ross, A. (2003). Die Gunst des kantigen Kinns [online]. *Spiegel Online*. Retrieved from http://www.spiegel.de/unispiegel/jobundberuf/bewerbungsfotos-die-gunst-des-kantigen-kinns-a-262041.html

Tomorrow Focus [online] FOCUS Online Video-Serie: Das Vorstellungsgespräch, Folge 6: „Warum sollten wir Sie einstellen?". Retrieved from http://www.tomorrow-focus.de/jobs-karriere/artikel/focus-online-video-serie-das-vorstellungsgespraech-folge-6-warum-sollten-wir-sie-einstellen_aid_554.html

17 How to: preparing to find a job as a Spanish teacher in the UK

Gemma Carmen Belmonte Talero[1]

1.   Introduction

This case study is about the design of the one-day course 'How to find a job as a Spanish teacher in the UK', which is taught at the Instituto Cervantes in London. The course came to exist due to a large number of requests from Spaniards who have come to the UK in recent years – many of them wanting to find a job as a Spanish teacher – and realising that they lacked the knowledge as to how to go about it. Most of the course participants have been Spanish graduates from different fields of study but there have also been an increasing number of participants from Latin America.

Course participants often point out that when it comes to retraining or acquiring a new job specialisation, the information found on the internet can appear overwhelming and for them – mostly newcomers to the teaching profession – having a friendly face who can guide them through the vast amounts of information available is very useful. Likewise, the course facilitator offers a key support as participants experience the challenges, joys and frustrations of the job search. Many need support to boost their confidence.

Keywords: Spanish, teacher, skills, job market.

1. Instituto Cervantes, London, United Kingdom; gemma.belmonte@cervantes.es

How to cite this chapter: Belmonte Talero, G. C. (2016). How to: preparing to find a job as a Spanish teacher in the UK. In E. Corradini, K. Borthwick and A. Gallagher-Brett (Eds), *Employability for languages: a handbook* (pp. 117-120). Dublin: Research-publishing.net. http://dx.doi.org/10.14705/rpnet.2016.cbg2016.472

2. What we did

After being given the required permission to go ahead with the running of the course, the main rationale that helped to create a useful and attractive course was to place oneself in the course participants' shoes in order to foresee their main needs and requirements as newcomers to the UK who hoped to access a very specific job market.

A helpful method for the organisation of the course has been to structure it in three parts: 1) greetings and introductions, 2) generic knowledge about the UK job market, and 3) specific knowledge about teaching Spanish in different UK educational contexts, such as early years, primary, secondary, further education, higher education and as a more freelance activity (i.e. au-pairing, private tutoring or organising language clubs, amongst others).

2.1. Greetings and introductions

This part of the course is actually crucial in that it helps the group to take shape and it creates a trusting atmosphere in which it is possible to share personal information and expectations within the group. By hearing about individuals' goals and previous experiences, course participants actually begin to clarify their own aspirations in the process of reinventing themselves (Clark, 2013). Here, 'adaptability' is explored as a key skill to have for the workforce and, through an open forum, participants share their concerns and the obstacles that they have overcome so far in the job search process.

2.2. Generic knowledge about the UK job market

Here, great emphasis is placed on the cultural clashes that may be encountered when Mediterranean, Latin and Anglo-Saxon cultures come into contact, especially in business contexts. Practical examples are provided in order to illustrate the explanations given, often referring to the tutor's and to the participants' past life experiences. In this sense, reference to the cultural values and dimensions that influence workplace communication help to illustrate the points made in a more objective and successful way (Hofstede, Hofstede, & Minkov, 2010).

Content covered at this stage refers to the characteristics of the UK job market; the job skills that UK employers prefer; raising awareness of the so-called hidden job market; and acquiring strategies for improving visibility by exposure to new opportunities, like-minded people and useful networks.

2.3. Specific knowledge about teaching Spanish in different UK educational contexts

In this part of the course, we analyse the idiosyncrasies of teaching at different stages and in different educational environments, considering what works and what does not work when looking for jobs in each sector (Prospects, 2015). We also cover content referring to the legal requirements within the teaching profession, such as the Disclosure and Barring Service (DBS) checks or the Qualified Teacher Status (QTS), and also include a section on the accreditation and recognition of foreign degrees. More entrepreneurial aspects of the job search are also explored, such as registering oneself as self-employed, undertaking consultancy work, working for language and teaching agencies or fulfilling tax responsibilities.

Additionally, throughout the course we critically analyse a selection of resources, such as job advertisements, institutional websites, etc. from which essential keywords and attributes are highlighted for their relevance in the job application process.

3.   Discussion of outcomes

Since 2011, the course has run on 26 occasions and it has enrolled 335 participants. The feedback received has been very positive, often highlighting the fact that the course exceeded the attendees' expectations. A follow-up course is being designed in order to further the knowledge covered regarding the search process for Spanish teaching posts in the UK, in which more specific references to Latin American idiosyncrasies will be explored. Likewise, participants' feedback forms have highlighted the usefulness of considering this course as a forum for discussing their personal interests. In this sense, an interesting follow-up is the creation of a blog in order to offer more opportunities for the participants' exchange of information once the course is finished.

4. Conclusion

Graduates often need further support in understanding how generic employability skills suit particular jobs. In this regard, this course has become an important step in the learning of employability skills in order to become Spanish teachers in the UK. In the case study explored here, the course participants have come from Spain and Latin America. Such a course would also be beneficial for other nationality groups with similar professional interests, for example Chinese individuals wanting to become Chinese language teachers in the UK.

References and links

Clark, D. (2013). *Reinventing you: define your brand, imagine your future* [video]. Talks at Google. Retrieved from https://www.youtube.com/watch?v=hEeXeblddSo

Hofstede, G., Hofstede, G. J., & Minkov, M. (2010). *Cultures and organizations. Software of the mind* (3rd ed.). New York: McGraw-Hill.

Prospects. (2015). *Getting a teaching job* [online]. Retrieved from http://www.prospects.ac.uk/getting_a_teaching_job.htm

Section 3.

Bringing the workplace into the classroom

18 SOS employability: a support structure for language students

Eleanor Quince[1], James Minney[2], Charlotte Medland[3], and Francesca Rock[4]

Abstract

It is readily recognised that "study and residence abroad are significant contexts for second language learning and development" (Mitchell, Tracy-Ventura, & McManus, 2015, p. 1), but the Year Abroad (YA) also provides Modern Foreign Language (MFL) students with a unique opportunity to develop personal and professional skills. YA students go through what is often termed a 'transformative experience' (British Academy/UCML, 2012). However, the problem of skills self-recognition and articulation remains. Without strong support structures students struggle to understand these skills and how to talk about them. This case study explores the creation of an employability-focussed support structure for MFL undergraduate students centred on preparing for, getting the most out of, and articulating the 'soft skills' learnt from the YA. The study presents evidence from three core activities: 1) interviews with YA returners, now final-year students; 2) support through tailored employability modules; and 3) the launch of an interactive online resource for students who are on their YA.

Keywords: year abroad, transformative, employability, skills development, reflection, languages.

1. University of Southampton, Southampton, United Kingdom; E.M.Quince@soton.ac.uk

2. University of Southampton, Southampton, United Kingdom; J.D.Minney@soton.ac.uk

3. University of Southampton, Southampton, United Kingdom; C.J.Medland@soton.ac.uk

4. University of Southampton, Southampton, United Kingdom; F.Rock@soton.ac.uk

How to cite this chapter: Quince, E., Minney, J., Medland, C., & Rock, F. (2016). SOS employability: a support structure for language students. In E. Corradini, K. Borthwick and A. Gallagher-Brett (Eds), *Employability for languages: a handbook* (pp. 123-132). Dublin: Research-publishing.net. http://dx.doi.org/10.14705/rpnet.2016.cbg2016.473

1.   Context and rationale

The very nature of the YA – unfamiliar surroundings, distance from friends and relatives, change in work/study culture – means that students need to adapt and assimilate quickly.

Recent 'skills lists', issued by bodies such as the Council for Industry and Higher Education (AGR/CIHE, 2011), draw attention to a variety of complex 'soft skills' which employers look for in potential employees: confidence, initiative, resilience, flexibility, self-motivation/drive. These skills are often categorised as 'personal skills' and, as they tend to be developed through 'experience', can be very difficult for students to master (Havergal, 2015). This difficulty is further compounded by the struggle to readily define and identify the skills: what is 'resilience'?; how does someone know that they are 'resilient'?; – and the problem of articulation – how do you evidence 'resilience' in your CV, personal statement, or at an interview? Students feel more confident talking about their academic achievements rather than their personal skills.

Students' time abroad accelerates their professional development alongside their language proficiency. Staff comment on the change: YA returners are more confident, engaged, and receive criticism more readily; in essence, they have begun to develop the skills employers are looking for, and the YA acts as evidence of this. However, the problem of skills self-recognition and articulation remains (Leggott & Stapleford, 2004; Small & Deakin Crick, 2008). Without strong support structures, students struggle to understand these skills and how to talk about them.

To overcome this, researchers and students at the University of Southampton have established a framework to support MFL students in advance of, and on return from, the YA:

- First, interviews with returning YA students established how confident they were about presenting their professional development.

- Second, the results of these interviews informed the creation of two Employability Modules and an employability-focussed online resource, responding to the problem of skills self-recognition and articulation. The Year Two employability module encourages the use of an e-portfolio to record and articulate skills developed through experience, an activity which can be continued during the YA and implemented through the Final Year module.

- Third, the Residence and Employment Abroad Leading to International Employability (REALIE) website provides peer-to-peer support, advice and links to resources, including monthly blogs by current YA students – selected from an open application round.

2. Aims and objectives

The overarching aim of this initiative was the creation of an employability-focussed support structure for undergraduate MFL students.

The objectives of the initiative are to:

- assess feedback from YA returners on the soft skills they feel they have developed during the YA;

- identify common issues centred around articulating soft skills development;

- prepare students for soft skills development during the YA through the provision of tailored employability modules;

- create a framework for reflection on and articulation of these skills;

- facilitate students' awareness of the transferability of these skills into the graduate job market.

3.   What we did

3.1.   Information gathering,
interviews with Year Abroad Returners

The MFL students interviewed had completed YA internships in France
and Mexico and had had the opportunity to develop 'soft skills' in a work
environment. It was apparent that until they were interviewed for this project
they had not reflected on that development. They were aware of soft skills and
the importance of these during the recruitment process and in the workplace, but
needed prompting to identify them. However, the students had clearly reflected
on residence abroad as a generally transformative experience.

Unsurprisingly, the students focused on communication skills as those which
they felt had developed most during their YA. This was not restricted to making
progress in the foreign language. As their principal objective whilst abroad
was to develop their foreign language skills, the students had paid particular
attention to language and its use. By observing and listening to colleagues – 'soft
skills' in themselves – students had gained insight into more subtle aspects of
communication and how communication impacts on the creation of a positive
working environment. The students also felt they were in a privileged position;
colleagues spoke more freely around them. One student commented that she
"knew all the gossip" and that her colleagues sometimes seemed to forget she
was there when discussing work related issues. The reasons for this are unclear:
perhaps an underestimation of the students' understanding or possibly because
the students were not perceived as full members of the team, being short-term
employees.

This sensitivity to language also provided opportunity for broader cultural
observations, for example, regarding formality and politeness in the workplace
and the relationship between this and professional hierarchy. Students commented
that their work environments seemed more formal than those in the UK, but
acknowledged that their experience of comparable UK environments was limited.
Conversely, one student completing an internship in Mexico contrasted the

formality she noted in some aspects of her work environment with an exuberant friendliness and what she perceived as a good number of colleagues' desire to do "as little as possible". While noting these cultural differences, students stressed that these were personal observations and did not necessarily extend to other workplaces. It was apparent that the students had become sophisticated cultural observers and that – as they noted – this recognition of cultural difference had a profound and positive impact upon them. On return from the YA, they felt more open to other cultures and had become increasingly flexible in their personal and professional attitudes, and more accommodating to others in team-working environments.

Finally, the most significant effect of residence abroad was a greater willingness to take on challenges and an improved ability to overcome them. The students saw the YA itself as a positive but challenging experience, and, having overcome many individual challenges while abroad, they were more confident, resilient and independent. They also saw the practical side to this ability: being able to plan, prioritise, and self-set deadlines – effectively to project manage – underpinned by the confidence that they could achieve, as one student said, anything she set her mind to. Interestingly, the students struggled to give specific examples of how the skills developed had led them to work/behave differently since returning, but rather felt that the experience had impacted on every aspect of their personal, academic and professional lives.

3.2. The provision of tailored employability modules to prepare students for soft skills development during the YA

The interview results were combined with research into the employment challenges faced by Humanities students (AGR, 2013; HESA, 2014). Three key aims were identified to support the skills development of MFL undergraduates:

- Students must learn to recognise how they are developing soft skills, and which skills they are developing, *before* they leave for their YA.

- This learning must be self-determined, to ensure that students are able to continue while away from campus.

- Students must be aware of how their YA skills transfer into the graduate job market (British Academy/UCML, 2012).

The second year employability module was created during summer 2015 to facilitate the first and second aims. Through the second year module, MFL students are encouraged to step outside their comfort zone and try new activities, including internships. The first session focusses on e-portfolios, used to facilitate independent reflection on skills development. Students learn about e-portfolios on a conceptual level, alongside why they should use them (Yorke & Knight, 2006). E-portfolios enhance students' awareness of their learning in relation to skills rather than grades, encouraging them to link skills with experience and to evidence development through various media – blogs; photography; videos; social networks. Students are shown a demonstration of how to setup the preferred e-portfolio, Pathbrite (www.pathbrite.com), and a number of Pathbrite 'case studies', created by current undergraduate Humanities students, evidence how the e-portfolio can work with students' curricular, co-curricular, and extra-curricular activity. In subsequent sessions students are set tasks to help build their e-portfolio, motivating them and encouraging increased self-awareness. Moreover, MFL students are encouraged to continue building e-portfolio content during their YA, creating an evidence base for job applications and interviews on their return. All e-portfolio activity is supported by a 'Resources and Advice' page in the module's Virtual Learning Environment (VLE) and a dedicated postgraduate teaching assistant.

The final aim – that MFL students must be aware of how their YA skills transfer into the graduate job market – is achieved through the module VLE. The site houses information which helps students to gauge 'What employers want', including internal and external resources, provided by the University Careers Service, The Guardian, TargetJobs and Milkround. The VLE also hosts links to skills-building resources, based on the transferable skills list on the University's Opportunity Profiles 'OPUS' website (http://opus.soton.ac.uk), demystifying such terms as 'resilience' while helping MFL students to understand how they demonstrate their skills. A collection of work experience, volunteering, and internship opportunities encourage students to get off-campus experience before their YA, in order to build confidence in existing abilities, such as communication with people from different cultures and backgrounds.

3.3. The creation of a framework for reflection and articulation on YA-developed skills through the launch of an interactive online resource for students

The REALIE website was created in 2012 by the Centre for Languages, Linguistics and Area Studies (LLAS) and the Modern Languages Department at the University of Southampton. During summer 2015, the Faculty employability team undertook to update the REALIE site, creating an interactive employability resource for undergraduate students embarking on a YA. An MFL student partner was recruited to redesign and develop the website before re-launching REALIE at the start of the 2015/16 academic year.

REALIE provides information for MFL students before, during, and after the YA. It helps students to identify, develop and demonstrate skills gained whilst studying and/or working overseas by highlighting how the YA experience can be used to develop skills and increase employability. Resources are tailored specifically to the three YA choices: English Language Assistant for the British Council; studying at a partner university as an ERASMUS student; or on a work placement. In order to create a resource which is both interactive and student-led, a blogging platform was incorporated into the REALIE site. Via the blog, a selection of current third year MFL students share their experiences, advice, and the skills they develop throughout their time abroad. Bloggers are able to reflect on their own growing skillset whilst sharing information and advice with their peers.

In the first semester, YA bloggers share their experiences on the 'culture shock', the challenges they face and how they overcome them, and the skills they develop personally, professionally, and socially. Each blogger shares personal perspectives, focussing on skills development and employability. In the first few months abroad, bloggers noted developments in their communication, networking, project management, self-management and personal effectiveness skills. As one REALIE blogger reported: "We are developing our organisational skills like never before, completing tasks that are not dissimilar to the sort of challenges we'll have to one day face in the workplace". Furthermore, students working abroad have highlighted the differences in foreign working culture: a female blogger stated that she has learnt "to speak up without being afraid to do so in a new environment".

REALIE has been created by students, for students and will soon feature a new reflective tool to consolidate the site's aims. Designed for both REALIE bloggers and YA students, this tool will encourage them to think about the professional transition they are undergoing during their YA, how this has developed, and the ways in which it will become useful in future employment.

4.   Discussion and conclusion

This case study has identified that MFL students are greatly advantaged by their YA in the acceleration of their professional skills development, but that they do not always recognise this development as directly related to their employability. The creation of the Year Two Employability Module and the REALIE web resource facilitate a gradual, escalating awareness of the professional boost that a YA can give undergraduate students, encouraging self-reflection and bespoke growth. Bringing a student's existing achievements and skills together using Pathbrite gives them confidence in their personal as well as linguistic abilities, which in turn encourages them to make the most of the YA from the start.

Future work to enhance MFL employability will include case studies from students who have been REALIE bloggers, and reflection interviews with YA returners who have engaged with REALIE and the Year Two module, to gauge impact across the pilot year. Feedback from interviews and case studies, along with input from MFL colleagues and careers staff, will contribute to further development of YA employability support over summer 2016 and the creation of a final-year employability module.

References and links

AGR. (2013). The AGR Graduate Recruitment Survey 2013: Winter Review. *Association of Graduate Recruiters*. Retrieved from http://www.agr.org.uk/write/Documents/Surveys/The_AGR_Graduate_Recruitment_Survey_2013_Winter_Review.pdf

AGR/CIHE. (2011). Global Graduates into Global Leaders. *Association of Graduate Recruiters (AGR) and Council for Industry and Higher Education (CIHE)*.

British Academy/UCML. (2012). *Valuing the year abroad*. Position Paper.

Havergal, C. (2015). UK engagement survey: universities have limited impact on students' 'soft' skill development. *Times Higher Education*. Retrieved from https://www.timeshighereducation.com/news/uk-engagement-survey-universities-have-limited-impact-students-soft-skill-development

HESA. (2014). 2012/13 UK performance indicators – Employment of graduates. *Higher Education Statistics Agency*. Retrieved from https://www.hesa.ac.uk/pr/3271-press-release-206

Leggott, D., & Stapleford, J. (2004). Enhancing student awareness of employability skills through the use of progress files [online]. Leeds Metropolitan University. Retrieved from https://www.llas.ac.uk/resources/paper/2279#toc_0

Mitchell, R., Tracy-Ventura, N., & McManus, K. (2015). *Social interaction, identity and language learning during residence abroad*. EuroSLA, the European Second Language Association. Retrieved from http://www.eurosla.org/eurosla-monograph-series-2/social-interaction-identity-and-language-learning-during-residence-abroad/

REALIE: Residence and Employment Aboard, Leading to International Employability. Retrieved from http://www.realie.org

Small, T., & Deakin Crick, R. (2008). *Learning and self-awareness: an enquiry into personal development in higher education. The ViTaL Development & Research Programme Report No. 8*. University of Bristol. Retrieved from http://learningemergence.net/wp-content/uploads/2014/02/ViTaL_RDP_Report_08.pdf

Yorke, M., & Knight, P. T. (2006). Learning & employability series one: embedding employability into the curriculum [online]. *The Higher Education Academy*. Retrieved from http://www.employability.ed.ac.uk/documents/Staff/HEABriefings/ESECT-3-Embedding_employability_into_curriculum.pdf

19 Is developing employability skills relevant to adult language students?

Tita Beaven[1]

1.   Introduction

Open University (OU) students are typically mature students who combine studying part-time with work or caring responsibilities; the average age of OU language students has been dropping, and about 30% of our new students are now under 25.

The traditional view of adult learners who study languages is that they often study for pleasure or personal development, rather than for clear career goals. The current study investigated whether adult students found the development of employability skills as part of their language courses useful, and, if so, the development of which particularly key employability skills they valued most.

Keywords: adult learners, motivation, aspiration, survey.

2.   What we did

This study aimed at understanding the views languages students at the Open University have on employability, and if and how they think their language modules should equip them to develop/practise/enhance employability skills (Pegg, Waldock, Hendy-Isaac, & Lawton, 2012).

1. The Open University, Milton Keynes, United Kingdom; tita.beaven@open.ac.uk

How to cite this chapter: Beaven, T. (2016). Is developing employability skills relevant to adult language students? In E. Corradini, K. Borthwick and A. Gallagher-Brett (Eds), *Employability for languages: a handbook* (pp. 133-138). Dublin: Research-publishing.net. http://dx.doi.org/10.14705/rpnet.2016.cbg2016.474

Along with two colleagues[2], I conducted two surveys in 2015 amongst two cohorts of students enrolled in language courses at the Open University. The first cohort (127 responses) involved students enrolled on the module *Exploring languages and cultures*, the compulsory Level 1 (L1) module for all students on the BA (Hons) Language Studies. This BA includes strands in French, German, Spanish, and English (Applied Linguistics), and students specialise in any two of those strands. The module *Exploring languages and cultures* is taught in English and introduces key concepts relating to languages, language learning, plurilingualism and intercultural communication. The second cohort (259 responses) was made up of students of French, German or Spanish studying at Level 2 (L2), i.e. those who had typically already completed at least 120 credits at Level 1.

The survey was designed to find out the aspirations and motivations of adult language students with reference to the NUS/CBI (2011) definition of employability skills as encompassing: a positive attitude, self-management, teamworking, problem solving, communication and literacy, application of IT, application of numeracy, entrepreneurship and business, and customer awareness.

3.   Discussion of outcomes

In terms of motivation for studying languages, the study showed that although around a third of students study for personal development (L1: 37.4%, L2: 33.9%), overall the main motivation is to help them change or develop their career (L1: 44.7%, L2:33.5%); see Figure 1. Although the picture is not straightforward in the sense that students do not always study modules in a linear way, it also appears that students enrolled on the L1 module are more motivated by their career than those at level 2, and that the profile of students is changing. One has to remember that because students study part-time, and it typically takes students 6-8 years to complete a degree course, these changes between L1 and L2 might indicate a medium-term change rather than a more arbitrary difference in cohorts.

---

2. María Fernandez Toro and Concha Furnborough

Figure 1.   Students' main motivation for studying languages

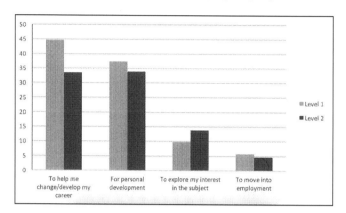

If students are partly motivated by changing or developing their career, how do their current occupations compare to their career aspirations? The results indicate that students are keen to move away from jobs in the areas of administrative and secretarial work, caring leisure and related services, and sales and customer service, and that they are aspiring to join the teaching profession or to become translators, interpreters, and communications specialists, as shown in Figure 2.

Figure 2.   Students' main current occupation vs. aspirations after study

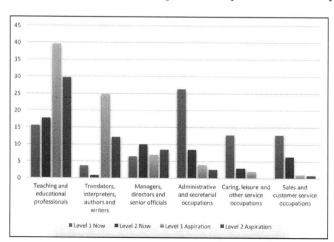

Most students felt that the qualification they were studying would be useful for their career, and thought that the most useful skills for their future profession would be communication and literacy (41.2%) and self-management (27.5%), followed by positive attitudes and team working (10.1 and 6.3% respectively).

Whilst it is not surprising that communication and literacy are considered the most useful skills amongst language students (Figure 3), self-management is perhaps a more unexpected choice, in particular as there is a marked increase in the usefulness accorded to this skill from L1 to L2 (21.1% and 34% respectively). Self-management involves "readiness to accept responsibility, flexibility, resilience, self-starting, appropriate assertiveness, time management, readiness to improve own performance based on feedback and reflective learning" (NUS/ CBI, 2011, p. 13) – all key to successful study, particularly at a distance and part-time – so this perhaps explains how the more experienced L2 students value the skill more, and are more aware of it.

Figure 3.   Most useful employability skill in your future profession

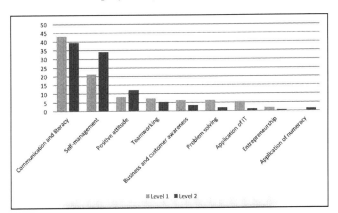

Students also thought it was important that some employability skills are included in future courses as we develop or update the curriculum, presumably even if not directly relevant to their career development. The most useful ones, again perhaps not surprisingly, being communication and literacy, followed by positive attitude, self-management, teamworking and problem solving (Figure 4).

Figure 4.   Usefulness of including these skills in our future language courses

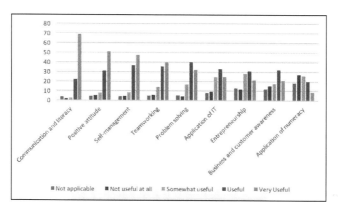

4.   Conclusion

This study revealed that, far from being mostly interested in studying languages for personal development, adult, part-time language students at the OU are keen to use their qualification to help them develop or change their career, and consider the qualification they are studying useful in achieving these goals.

Students were able to identify the most useful employability skills in their future career development, highlighting communication and literacy and self-management. However, they were also keen to see other skills, such as a positive attitude, teamwork and problem solving explicitly addressed in language courses in the future.

Although it might seem obvious that communication and literacy are the most valued skills by language students, this might also indicate a blurring between employability skills and the actual subject knowledge that is developed through a degree in languages. Whilst responding to the professional aspirations of students in the way we develop our curriculum, as language educators we should also be clear about what constitutes generic employability skills versus content specific knowledge and skills that are developed by studying languages. Debates about employability, especially in language education, should reflect the tensions between developing a knowledge curriculum and fostering the development of more generic skills.

References and links

NUS/CBI. (2011). *Working towards your future: making the most of your time in higher education.* Retrieved from http://www.nus.org.uk/Global/CBI_NUS_Employability%20 report_May%202011.pdf

Pegg, A., Waldock, J., Hendy-Isaac, S., & Lawton, R. (2012). *Pedagogy for employability.* York: Higher Education Academy. Retrieved from https://www.heacademy.ac.uk/sites/ default/files/pedagogy_for_employability_update_2012.pdf

20 Up-skilling through e-collaboration

Saskia Huc-Hepher[1] and Elsa Huertas Barros[2]

Abstract

This paper presents an e-collaboration project involving real-time video-conferencing exchanges between students from the University of Westminster and the Université Catholique de Lille. Students drew on diverse resources, including written quantitative data and first-hand qualitative data in French/English to complete weekly tasks. Follow-up work was an integral component of the co-project, taking the form of a series of adaptations in French/English based on the source materials studied and the knowledge of the intercultural issues explored collaboratively. These adaptations, which ensured the development of wider employability expertise, ranged from professional reports to newspaper articles, and from conference papers to information leaflets.

Keywords: e-collaboration, employability, e-portfolio, modern foreign languages, task-based approach, transferable skills, translation education, virtual learning environments.

1.   Context and rationale

The creation of the European Higher Education Area (EHEA) in 1999 has given rise to a closer relationship between training and the labour market in Higher Education (HE). The EHEA prioritises a competence-based training approach,

---

1. University of Westminster, London, United Kingdom; S.V.Huc-Hepher@westminster.ac.uk

2. University of Westminster, London, United Kingdom; e.huertasbarros@westminster.ac.uk

How to cite this chapter: Huc-Hepher, S., & Huertas Barros, E. (2016). Up-skilling through e-collaboration. In E. Corradini, K. Borthwick and A. Gallagher-Brett (Eds), *Employability for languages: a handbook* (pp. 139-148). Dublin: Research-publishing.net. http://dx.doi.org/10.14705/rpnet.2016.cbg2016.475

139

building on the premise that learning is transferred to the workplace. In this new education paradigm, the development of transferable competences is vital to equip students with skills which enhance their employability. Employability has thus become a key concept in EU universities, as has the need to embed it in the modern language curriculum. Although recent research in the fields of languages and translation unequivocally demonstrates the value of foreign language knowledge on the graduate labour market, employers are increasingly seeking additional abilities including: intercultural, interpersonal and communication skills, aptitude at addressing international audiences, peer-review competence, adaptability, business awareness, subject knowledge and research skills (Chouc & Calvo, 2011; Lisaité et al., 2016).

In recent decades, innovative pedagogical approaches have emerged in foreign language teaching and translator education in HE. Since the late 80s and 90s, traditional product-oriented and teacher-centred 'transmissionist' methodologies have been replaced by authentic and collaborative approaches that consider students – and learning itself – as the main agents of the learning process (González Davies, 2004; Hurtado Albir, 1999/2003; Kiraly, 2000; Nunan, 1989). Interpersonal competence, and particularly collaborative learning, is therefore a paramount transferable skill for the language and translation graduates of the 21st century. In this new education context, pedagogic tasks and projects that imitate professional assignments should be embedded in the languages curriculum so that students engage in "real-life" activities that are representative of professional standards (González Davies, 2004, p. 19).

Collaborative learning approaches, including task-based (González Davies, 2004; Hurtado Albir, 1999/2003; Nunan, 1989) and social constructivist approaches (Kiraly, 2000) favour students' active involvement and mutual support as well as a positive interaction between students with different backgrounds, cultures and learning styles. Students construct knowledge together "through meaningful interactions with peers" (Kiraly, 2000, p. 60), and the tutor acts as a facilitator assisting students during the learning process, which effectively encourages students to take control and ownership of their learning. With the prevalence of Information and Communication Technology (ICT), HE is undergoing a digital revolution, resulting in improved interactions between students, tutors and the subject. The development of digital environments in recent years, particularly e-collaboration and communication tools, has undeniably enhanced foreign-language learning and teaching through Virtual Learning Environments (VLEs) in student-centred classes. Using Web-based learning platforms, tutors now have access to a wide range of tools to facilitate language learning for students, which complements the more traditional classroom-based setting. It is on this theoretical backdrop that the following case study was conducted.

2.   Aims and objectives

The principal objective of the e-collaboration between the universities of Westminster and Lille was to incorporate employability into the core of a final-year, 15-credit, French for Work module through a series of tasked-based, online sessions. The timing of the module, towards the end of the UK students' undergraduate programmes, helped to prepare students for life beyond academia, serving as a bridge between the worlds of HE and work. Similarly, as a proportion of the UK students had not spent time in a French-speaking country during their degree, the module aimed to provide them with valuable exposure to authentic spoken French in spontaneous, real-time situations. The final overarching objective of the co-project was to equip BA French Translation students with the creative adaptation skills increasingly required in the globalised context of contemporary communication.

In more specific terms, the e-collaboration aimed to enhance:

- intercultural awareness;

- transferable interpersonal skills;

- awareness of real-world 'transcreation' (a form of adaptation involving prioritisation, condensation, translation and localisation) remits and workplace contexts;

- peer review and critical reflection;

- contemporary/authentic foreign-language vocabulary;

- foreign-language receptive and productive skills;

- transferable data-mining and synthesis abilities;

- student-centred learning;

- register sensitivity;

- professional IT skills;

- coordinated working towards mutual deadlines;

- interdisciplinarity (the Lille participants majoring in law).

3. What we did

3.1. Overview of the e-collaboration project

As stipulated in the Westminster module description, the main topics serving as the thematic framework for the co-project were 'globalisation', 'human rights' and 'technology in society'. The collaboration involved a series of online synchronous (i.e. real-time) and a-synchronous sessions (i.e. staggered between Westminster and Lille), convened in dedicated language laboratories, equipped with PCs, integrated cameras, headphones and microphones. Westminster's Blackboard VLE was used as the database for the shared learning materials, the platform for uploading student outputs, and the mechanism for live videoconferencing (via Blackboard Collaborate). Each week, students were instructed to work on a topical sub-theme relevant to both the French and UK socio-cultural, political and legal contexts, as well as corresponding to the three designated module themes. Particular topics were selected for their potential to provoke debate and inspire intercultural reflection (see Section 3.2. for samples).

Students were presented with a balance of French and English online resources to inform their thinking and subsequent critical positioning. This ensured that students at both institutions had an awareness of the cultural, legal and ideological peculiarities of each other's national contexts. Likewise, a variety of sources was chosen to expose students to different registers, modes and text-types, thereby challenging their ability to understand, assimilate, synthesise and adapt multiple forms of data. Examples of sources consulted include: authentic videoclips; raw quantitative data (e.g. online survey results); national radio podcasts; newspaper articles; and legislation. Having spent time studying these materials individually and making notes of key points, students were placed in small groups in Blackboard's Virtual Classroom, where they discussed several aspects of the topic in virtual 'face-to-face' interactions, guided by pre-established tutor suggestions.

As the purpose of the synchronous conferences was not only to give students cultural insights and exposure to authentic spoken French/English but to also provide an additional source of qualitative data for follow-up adaptation tasks, Westminster students were asked to complete a Student Debriefing Form after each session. The form allowed students to log the specific topic discussed, the sub-themes explored, French and English ideological/cultural/legislative differences, a general summary of the conversation and conclusions drawn, together with noteworthy linguistic features and/or vocabulary. This written record was subsequently consulted by students to consolidate their learning and facilitate direct quotation of the French students, thereby increasing the credibility of their professionalised transcreations through the use of first-hand evidence.

3.2. Description of transcreation tasks

In accordance with the Westminster host module description, the e-collaboration was framed in terms of professional simulations. A distinct scenario-based task was therefore set each week, requiring students to produce a transcreation according to a professional brief. Particular remits were embedded in a variety of work-related settings, and as such necessitated independent research into the appropriate register of language, format and structure to meet the expectations of the audience targeted. Each adaptation involved: managing a variety of bilingual sources; prioritising and re-appropriating relevant information for their purposes; understanding a range of registers, accents and modes; transferring information from and into French/English; condensing multiple data into a clear and concise document; and producing a coherent target text (200 words) consistent with the norms of the professional environment specified. Adaptation tasks ranged from reports, set in corporate or political contexts, to newspaper articles, and from academic conference papers to information leaflets. Below are several concrete examples of briefs devised for the co-project:

1) You work at the Agence France-Presse international news agency and have been asked to write a short **press release** in French on the recent publication of a book on the selfie phenomenon, *Tous selfie ! Pourquoi tous accro ?* by Pauline Escande-Gauquié. Using information retrieved from the linked France Inter radio episode, together with any persuasive quotes noted during your conversation with the students in Lille, write a text in French which encourages journalists to take up the news item and publicise the book.

2) You work for France Inter in the 'Service Public' production team and have been asked to write the **presenter's introduction** to a forthcoming episode on the migrant 'jungle' in Calais. Based on information found in the three video clips viewed this week, and in response to the French students' audio files (posted on the discussion board), write a short script in French introducing the issue to listeners. Once you have drafted the script, play the role of the presenter and upload your recording to the Voice Board on Blackboard.

3) You work in the Communications Department of the EuropaNova think tank and have been asked to produce a **flyer** (in French) encouraging

members of the public to attend a debate you are hosting in Paris. The public debate has been organised in the aftermath of Paris's terrorist attacks and seeks grassroots' opinion on France's/Europe's fundamental ideals of free speech, free movement and equality for all. Your leaflet will be distributed to the general public prior to the debate and should give some legal and ideological context to the situation in France, as well as presenting arguments for and/or against changes to current legislation/ policy.

4) You are a prompt-writer with Red Bee Media, and France 2 have commissioned you to write an **autocue** in French about the ways in which the British and French governments are infringing the online privacy of their citizens. The autocue will be part of an editorial news feature to be broadcast in the 'Journal Télévisé de 20 heures'.

To conclude the module, and based on the material developed collaboratively, students were required to produce an independent project in French and English at a level broadly equivalent to CEFR C1. This project consisted of an e-portfolio comprising their three most successful adaptations in French (totalling 600 words), together with a covering email serving to introduce the dossier within another simulated professional context (see Project Brief 1 below). It also included an 800-word transcreation task into English (see Project Brief 2 below).

Project Brief 1: You are applying for an in-house transcreation position at World Writers and, as part of the recruitment process, have been asked to produce a portfolio of three texts in French, which you originally drafted within the framework of the Lille co-project. The company is looking to see how the process enhanced your data-mining and synthesis abilities, your intercultural awareness and language-transfer skills. You are also required to write a 200-word introductory email in French, providing the Transcreation Director and Recruitment Manager with background information on both the co-project itself and the texts chosen for the dossier, explaining why the e-collaboration and related tasks make you the ideal candidate for the transcreation position.

Project Brief 2: You are an academic specialising in contemporary French culture and society, and are keen to investigate further one of the sub-themes studied under the Lille Co-Project. The final output of your research will be a paper for the 2016 Annual Conference of the Association for the Study of Modern and Contemporary France (ASMCF), the overarching subject of which is 'Transitions'. Your paper should give insights into French legislation, policy and public opinion on the chosen issue, and should be presented within the framework of the conference theme. The specific title and angle of the paper is your choice, but incorporating a combination of first-hand evidence (from the Lille students) and your own desk research on the subject is desirable.

Your research will draw on information contained in the corresponding Student Debriefing Form and any relevant materials developed collaboratively online. In total, you are required to submit three French source texts – one of which must be a quantitative survey – which will inform the points made in your paper to support your main line of argumentation.

4.   Discussion and conclusion

Our case study demonstrates how the use of e-collaboration and transcreation tasks set within a range of simulated professional contexts can be integrated in the modern language curriculum to enhance students' employability. Building upon student-centred approaches successfully applied to the fields of languages and translation education (González Davies, 2004; Hurtado Albir, 1999/2003; Kiraly, 2000; Nunan, 1989), the co-project and scenario-based tasks enabled undergraduate language students to develop key transferable skills required in today's workplace. These include: language and communication competence, interpersonal skills, intercultural awareness, creative skills, information-mining ability, thematic competence, peer-review, synthesis skills and critical reflection.

Based on our experience and student feedback, e-collaboration has proven to be extremely valuable for the professional world. The implementation of e-learning and virtual collaboration is an effective tool that increases language students' motivation, fosters teamwork, and facilitates the incorporation of peer-learning as part of the teaching and learning equation. The specific language-based tasks and professional simulations devised within the e-collaboration framework built students' public-speaking confidence by helping them overcome reservations experienced in face-to-face exchanges. The co-project exposed students to new ICT and provided them with key technological skills needed to learn promptly and effectively to complete the designated tasks. Embedding the individual transcreations within the project (i.e. these marks counting to the overall module mark) was an effective mechanism to ensure active and regular participation.

Finally, organising the co-project so that students in both institutions were at the same level of study ensured they had equivalent language knowledge and understanding of the complex issues discussed.

In the words of a mature student who participated in the e-collaboration, it

"was excellent in enabling us to interact with the French students [...]. Whatever I find myself doing employment-wise, I have found [it] useful... The module tasks have enabled me to use skills from my previous employment but also to gain knowledge from other fields".

Another former student on the module added:

"I came to notice the importance of the techniques of adaptation and translation [...] whilst interning for the Austrian Embassy [...]. The skills I have acquired [...] helped me deliver efficient work in a fast and precise manner. Now that I work for an agency of the European Commission in Brussels, I appreciate even more [...] these various skills".

Overall, therefore, this case study has proved itself to be a credible, viable and replicable model for the enhancement of undergraduate modern language student employability.

References and links

Chouc, F., & Calvo, E. (2011). Embedding employability in the curriculum and building bridges between academia and the work-place: a critical analysis of two approaches. *La linterna del traductor: la revista multilingüe de Asetrad, 4,* 71- 86.

González Davies, M. (2004). *Multiple voices in the translation classroom. Activities, tasks and projects.* Amsterdam/Philadelphia: John Benjamins. Retrieved from http://dx.doi.org/10.1075/btl.54

Hurtado Albir, A. (1999/2003). *Enseñar a traducir. Metodología en la formación de traductores e intérpretes.* Madrid: Edelsa.

Kiraly, D. (2000). *A social constructivist approach to translator education. Empowerment from theory to practice.* Manchester: St. Jerome.

Lisaité, D., Maylath, B., Mousten, B., Valdez, S., Castel-Branco, M., Minacori, P., & Vandepitte, S. (2016). Negotiating meaning at a distance: peer feedback in electronic learning translation environments in the trans-atlantic and pacific project. In M. Thelen, G.-W. van Egdom, D. Verbeeck, & B. Lewandowska-Tomaszczyk (Eds.), *Translation and Meaning New Series, vol.1. Proceedings of the Maastricht Session of the 6th International Maastricht-Łódź Duo Colloquium on "Translation and Meaning",* Maastricht School of Translation and Interpreting, 21-22 May 2015. Berlin, Frankfurt am Main: Peter Lang.

Nunan, D. (1989). *Designing tasks for the communicative classroom.* Cambridge: Cambridge University Press.

21 The employability advantage: embedding skills through a university-wide language programme

Tiziana Cervi-Wilson[1] and Billy Brick[2]

1.   Introduction

In an ever unstable job market, improving the employability skills of graduates comes very high in the priorities of languages departments. As the employment of graduates appears among the performance indicators of institutions in higher education, universities are focussing more and more upon the development of employability related skills to enhance students' prospects in the job market.

All UK universities are measured on the first jobs that their students acquire after graduation. In response to this, Coventry University implemented numerous new strategies to emphasise and stress the importance of education for employability.

This chapter will report on the Institution-Wide Language Provision (IWLP) and its explicit link to the higher education employability agenda. IWLPs typically cater for students who want to study a language alongside their degree subject in addition to, or as part of, their main degree course. Uniquely, Coventry University offers language modules to undergraduate students as part of a scheme called Add+vantage. These modules are designed to embed employability into undergraduate courses, allowing students to demonstrate language skills and formal learning when entering the graduate job market. The Add+vantage modules are taught over an eleven-week semester, with the eleventh week solely dedicated to employability.

1. Coventry University, Coventry, United Kingdom; t.cervi@coventry.ac.uk

2. Coventry University, Coventry, United Kingdom; b.brick@coventry.ac.uk

How to cite this chapter: Cervi-Wilson, T., & Brick, B. (2016). The employability advantage: embedding skills through a university-wide language programme. In E. Corradini, K. Borthwick and A. Gallagher-Brett (Eds), *Employability for languages: a handbook* (pp. 149-153). Dublin: Research-publishing.net. http://dx.doi.org/10.14705/rpnet.2016.cbg2016.476

Keywords: institution-wide languages programme, IWLP, employability, languages, common European framework of reference for languages, CEFR.

2.   What we did

Students at Coventry University are given the chance each year to chose a credit-bearing employability module offered as part of the Add+vantage suite of modules. These modules focus primarily on a work experience and career development activities. This provides students with a unique opportunity to enhance their knowledge, skills and qualifications within a work-focussed environment. For example, students thinking of a career in volunteering can use their chosen Add+vantage module to volunteer in the community. For those who are planning to work in international contexts, the Add+vantage language modules enable them to demonstrate their language skills to potential employers.

In order to ensure quality, consistency, and to provide strategic vision, an advisory board was established to bring together representatives from the different departments/faculties involved in the scheme to gain consensus on issues such as commissioning and decommissioning modules, timetabling, registry, quality standards and general operational challenges. Furthermore, the advisory board decides whether modules are 'fit for purpose' by assessing whether they fulfil a number of employability-focussed criteria. The modules also ease the transition from university to work.

In selecting the range of employability competencies to be developed through the Add+vantage scheme, the university has adopted this definition:

> "Employability is a set of competencies that make graduates more likely to gain employment and be successful in their chosen occupation(s), which benefits themselves, the workforce, the community and the economy" (Yorke, 2006, p. 8).

The Add+vantage scheme offers a broad range of subject areas which are arranged in different themes. As detailed on the Coventry University's (2016) website, in the 'Global Languages' theme, students can learn French, German, Italian, Mandarin, Spanish, Arabic, Japanese or Portuguese. Included in 'Global Perspectives' are modules in which students learn how to do business in different parts of the world or look at intercultural communication in the global society. Under the 'Professional Development' category, modules have been created in association with local companies to give students unique industry insight and guidance for graduate recruitment. Other themes include Employer Engagement, Enterprise and Entrepreneurship, Work Experience/ Volunteering, Global Experience, Work-related Projects and Work-related Skills. The common thread is that they all develop and strengthen the skills employers are looking for and improve students' prospects of securing employment.

The languages element of the Add+vantage scheme at Coventry University is organised by the School of Humanities. This unique programme was launched in October 2006, and has greatly increased IWLP provision across the University.

Degree programmes normally require students to acquire 120 credits per academic year and ten of these must be selected from the Add+vantage suite of modules at each level. Classes are offered at absolute beginner, post-beginner and intermediate level, and dedicated business language modules are also available in French and Spanish. Students are also able to register as complete beginners at level one, two or three. The modules span 11 weeks for two hours per week and students are required to complete two in-class assessments: one in week five and the other in week ten. Students taking modules at levels two and three can use the credits to count towards their degree programmes. Classes are held in dedicated Add+vantage slots, which help to eradicate timetabling clashes, as the University stipulates that no other classes are to be scheduled for these slots. Enrolment, attendance monitoring and module changes are also centrally administered as part of the university's careers advice services.

A more recent development has seen the employability agenda more explicitly promoted by adding an extra week to the programme, in which tutors are required to encourage students to reflect upon how the module content supports and enhances career development and to deliver materials with a clear employability slant (Routes into Languages, 2015).

3.   Discussion of outcomes

Approximately 7,500 students take part in the programme which is repeated in both semesters. Of these around 3,000 choose to enrol on languages modules. Levels are explicitly mapped across to the Common European Framework of Reference for languages (CEFR) and each module is assessed in a similar way. Spanish and French continue to attract the most students, but over the last few years interest in Mandarin, Arabic and Japanese has expanded. As the modules are credit bearing, the school is funded directly from the centre, which is certainly a major factor in securing the programme's long-term success.

The range of personal and generic competencies incorporated in the Add+vantage scheme includes problem solving, action planning and organising, written/oral communication, and questioning and listening. In addition to these, further personal competencies are developed such as decisiveness, achievement orientation, initiative (creativity), self-confidence, influencing, adaptability, and reflectiveness.

4.   Conclusion

According to The Times (2014), Coventry University has increased its reputation for students' satisfaction and has since 2014 become a preferred students' destination for the modernity of its teaching.

This cannot be entirely attributed to the success of the Add+vantage programme, but it is certainly one of the contributing factors. By participating on the Add+vantage scheme, students can develop an increased awareness of the expectations of employers that are wider than mere academic competencies. Having the opportunity to develop comprehensive employability skills also enables students to contribute effectively in the workplace from day one or in their own business.

References and links

Coventry University. (2016). *Add+vantage*. Retrieved from http://www.coventry.ac.uk/study-at-coventry/student-support/enhance-your-employability/add-vantage/

Routes into Languages. (2015). *Employability* [online]. Retrieved from https://www.routesintolanguages.ac.uk/resources/library/languages-and-your-future

The Times. (2014, September 23). *Good university guide*. Retrieved from http://www.thetimes.co.uk/tto/education/gooduniversityguide/article4214708.ece

Yorke, M. (2006). Employability in higher education: what is – what is not. York: Higher Education Academy.

22 Spanish for business: a journey into employability

Amparo Lallana[1] and Victoria Pastor-González[2]

1.   Introduction

As language lecturers, we believe that we equip our graduates with a range of key skills that give them an edge in the employment market. But, query final year students of a Business and Languages degree on the value of language learning for employability, and they are likely to mention a small number of functional abilities such as CV writing and interview skills. This perception gap inspired us to critically assess how employability is embedded in our language modules. We started by identifying the most sought after skills amongst employers and then explored with the team how these skills are integrated and developed through tasks and assessments. Finally, matching skills and tasks, we visually modelled the process by which students acquire more complex skills as they become increasingly competent in the Target Language (TL).

Keywords: embedding employability skills, language learning, developmental model.

2.   What we did

In June 2015, Regent's University London (RUL) organised its first conference on languages and employability. This event triggered a series of questions within the Spanish teaching team. We knew that our graduates, 96% of whom are in full employment or further studies within six months of finishing their BA in

1. Regent's University London, London, United Kingdom; lallanaa@regents.ac.uk

2. Regent's University London, London, United Kingdom; pastorgonv@regents.ac.uk

How to cite this chapter: Lallana, A., & Pastor-González, V. (2016). Spanish for business: a journey into employability. In E. Corradini, K. Borthwick and A. Gallagher-Brett (Eds), *Employability for languages: a handbook* (pp. 155-160). Dublin: Research-publishing.net. http://dx.doi.org/10.14705/rpnet.2016.cbg2016.477

International Business, are attractive to employers. In addition to business subjects, our students enrol in one or two compulsory languages and complete a study period abroad, proof that the ability to speak other languages, coupled with international experience, gives graduates an extra edge in the current job market. However, following a number of informal conversations with our final year students, it became evident that although we, lecturers, were conscious of the range of employability skills that language learning provides, students lacked that awareness, and they were perhaps ill-equipped to transmit the value of this subject in a professional context.

To represent this perception gap that we believe affects students, lecturers and employers alike, we adopted the iceberg metaphor for culture. We then set out to explore ways in which we could evidence additional opportunities to develop hidden employability skills that learning a language provides in the context of our business degrees.

Figure 1.   Hidden employability skills

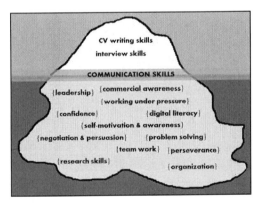

We used Figure 1 as a prompt for a brainstorming session with the team. We all agreed that the more visible functional skills – CV, cover letter, interview skills – are covered, but we then invited the team to identify how the other skills were explored and activated at different points of the curriculum, either as regular tasks or more importantly in the form of assessed work. We concluded that the development of employability in our language classes can be represented as a journey our learners embark upon, a journey simultaneous to the acquisition of the language. As language proficiency develops, different employability skills are practiced through more sophisticated tasks. Broadly speaking, employability is "making students aware of the world of work" (Daly, 2013, p. 5), and within this journey, students nurture this awareness as they progress through four developmental stages (see Figure 2).

Figure 2. A student's journey

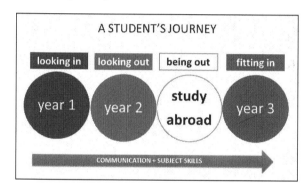

2.1. Year 1: looking in

In the first year, communication is basic and language mostly descriptive. Students talk about themselves and engage in a variety of simple tasks, such as applying for a job. In this task they learn vocabulary associated to departments and functions and identify specific skills for a particular department or post. They then reflect on their own skills and experiences to write a basic CV and cover letter to apply for authentic internship opportunities in the TL contexts. Finally, they prepare for the job interview, which constitutes the final oral assessment for these modules.

All along, students are looking in, exploring themselves as employable, and reflecting on what they have to offer to the world of work. Thus, skills such as self-awareness and basic interview skills are activated and practiced (Figure 3).

2.2.   Year 2: looking out

Students have by now gained relative proficiency and are able to communicate better and in more complex ways; they can offer opinions, present proposals and make recommendations; and they have the capacity to engage in tasks that look out into the TL cultural contexts and work practices. A key task in these modules is the research project. For this coursework, students research a question related to companies, work practices or the socioeconomic environment of their year abroad destination country(ies) and discuss their findings at different points in the semester through presentations and written exercises. With increasing language abilities, Year 2 students are now looking out, exploring new work environments and developing abilities such as presentation skills and problem-solving (Figure 3).

Figure 3.   Matching employability skills and language learning tasks in Years 1 and 2

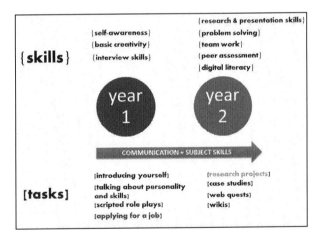

2.3.   Study abroad: being out

With full immersion and operating in the TL, linguistic ability develops significantly: from survival, to operational, to proficient. This compulsory Study

Abroad period also nurtures intercultural competence and awareness. Students have to adapt and react flexibly to new settings, new people, and new ways of doing things. During this rather challenging experience, most gain valuable skills such as resilience and confidence (Figure 4).

2.4. Year 3: fitting in

As illustrated in Figure 4, after the year abroad, language tasks seek to stimulate reflection on personal development and to enhance awareness of the knowledge and skills already gained through language learning and study abroad. Most importantly, students are actively thinking of their future employment, and are keen to demonstrate their fit in the world of work by engaging in more complex tasks that replicate real work environments and situations. One of such tasks is the negotiation where students discuss and agree the terms of a franchise contract.

With this assessment, students polish skills such as confidence and adaptability, but to succeed they must develop advanced skills such as persuasion and commercial awareness.

Figure 4.   Matching employability skills and language learning tasks in the Year Abroad and the Final Year

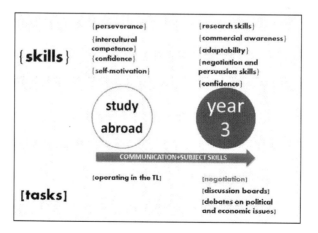

3.   Discussion of outcomes and conclusion

At institutions where employability is not a stand-alone element, this type of reflective exercise can be a strategy for language teams to consider how employability is embedded in the curriculum, identify possible gaps and develop a coordinated strategy. Ultimately, the objective is to create a coherent narrative, a story that students understand and are able to sell to future employers. For us, this is the next step; to come up with strategies – workshops, social media, printed material – to raise students' awareness of their journey into employability.

Reference and link

Daly, S. (2013). Enhancing employability skills through the use of film in the language classroom. *The Language Learning Journal*. Retrieved from http://dx.doi.org/10.1080/09571736.2013.779296

23 Learning by teaching: developing transferable skills

Sascha Stollhans[1]

1.   Introduction

Learning by teaching (German: *Lernen durch Lehren*, commonly abbreviated as *LdL*) is a teaching and learning approach which was developed by the French language teacher Jean-Pol Martin in German schools in the 1980s (Martin, 1985). The method sees students in the role of the teacher, and enhances their learning experience by encouraging them to teach other students and collaborate with fellow learners.

This case study presents an ongoing project in which second year students of German at the University of Nottingham plan, design and deliver a teaching session for first year beginners' students. The sessions are either carried out face-to-face or via video tutorials. This is an opportunity for the 'student teachers' to apply the knowledge they have acquired within the linguistics module *Fremdsprachen lernen und lehren* ('learning and teaching foreign languages') in a real-life context and to consolidate their own knowledge of German. The first year students, on the other hand, benefit from their peers' experience, knowledge and enthusiasm. By working on their projects, students have the opportunity to develop a number of transferable skills, such as teamwork, presentation and communication skills, and creativity.

Keywords: student engagement, collaboration, flipped classroom, computer-assisted language learning, ab initio language classes.

1. University of Nottingham, Nottingham, United Kingdom; sascha.stollhans@nottingham.ac.uk

How to cite this chapter: Stollhans, S. (2016). Learning by teaching: developing transferable skills. In E. Corradini, K. Borthwick and A. Gallagher-Brett (Eds), *Employability for languages: a handbook* (pp. 161-164). Dublin: Research-publishing.net. http://dx.doi.org/10.14705/rpnet.2016.cbg2016.478

2.   What I did

My second year module *Fremdsprachen lernen und lehren* ('learning and teaching foreign languages') introduces students to second language acquisition theories, and academic research into language teaching and learning. In order to bridge the gap between theory and practice, students work on a mid-term project in groups of two or three, during which they choose an aspect of the German language, research it and produce teaching materials for their fellow students on the German *ab initio* strand. They then either plan and deliver a lesson, or create a video tutorial. Before delivering their lessons or creating their videos, the plans are discussed in class with particular focus on the interface of linguistic theory and practice.

Both variants of the task require thorough research, consideration of theory and practical implications, and the development of clear explanations. Students are free to choose an approach which they consider appropriate (e.g. role-plays, demonstration of rules with the help of PowerPoint presentations, group activities, etc.). The face-to-face lessons are attended by both my colleague, who convenes the language module, and myself; the videos are integrated into the first year students' self-study programme. Some of the materials have also been used at the University of Sheffield. At the end of the project, students receive individual feedback.

Since we introduced the project for the first time during the academic year 2014/15, the outcomes have been very positive. Students have produced very creative and well thought-out materials, and students from both cohorts involved have enjoyed the project and benefited from it. For sample materials created by students, see Stollhans (2015).

3.   Discussion of outcomes

During the project, students are encouraged to develop a number of transferable skills. They work in teams on a collaborative project for which they need to structure content and present it in an accessible way. This requires, among others, IT skills, communication competencies, abstract thinking, problem-solving strategies, and creativity.

After the module ran in the academic year 2014/15, the 'student teachers' (N=27) were asked to evaluate the following statements about the activity using a five-point Likert scale (1 = strongly disagree; 5 = strongly agree):

- I enjoyed preparing and delivering the lesson. 4.36

- I got insight into the role of the teacher. 4.45

- Participating in this made me revise/consolidate certain aspects of the language myself. 4.18

- I would like to do something like this more often. 4.00

The overall very positive response to the project is also visible in the open comments, which include:

- "I was actually surprised at first by the fact that we were trusted to teach a class, especially first year students. It was a great idea, I enjoyed it a lot and everything went more or less as planned."

- "It was an opportunity for me to revise and test out what I had learned during the course (e.g. teaching methods), and I also gained some valuable experience teaching a foreign language to older students."

- "Mainly I learnt how to engage people in certain areas of language study and by flipping the role with me becoming the teacher, I had to learn what I was teaching in more detail and to be more accurate than I probably otherwise would have been."

These comments suggest that students also experienced that their confidence increased in the course of the project, as they were "trusted" with a significant and authentic 'real-life' task. Overall, the project was very successful, and it has become a regular feature of the module.

4.   Conclusion

This case study demonstrates how *learning by teaching* approaches can enable students to practise key employability skills, not just for teaching professions. Grzega and Schöner (2008) emphasise that by using *learning by teaching* methods,

> "learners are given the chance to acquire creativity, independence, self-confidence and key competencies, such as the ability to work in teams, the ability to communicate, complex thinking, the competence to seek and find information, explorative behaviour, presentation skills, project competence, Internet skills, the ability to structure information and generate knowledge, punctuality, reliability and patience" (p. 169).

All these skills are valuable assets for language graduates entering the job market. In conclusion, as one of the students phrased it in their open survey comment, "teaching is a very valuable and effective form of learning".

References and links

Grzega, J., & Schöner, M. (2008). The didactic model LdL (Lernen durch Lehren) as a way of preparing students for communication in a knowledge society. *Journal of Education for Teaching: International research and pedagogy, 34*(3), 167-175. Retrieved from http://dx.doi.org/10.1080/02607470802212157

Martin, J.-P. (1985). *Zum Aufbau didaktischer Teilkompetenzen beim Schüler.* Fremdsprachen-unterricht auf der lerntheoretischen Basis des Informationsverarbeitungsansatzes. Tübingen: Narr Verlag.

Stollhans, S. (2015). *"Flipped roles": German students as teachers.* University of Nottingham, School of Cultures, Languages and Area Studies, web blog. Retrieved from http://blogs.nottingham.ac.uk/clas/2015/05/21/flipped-roles-german-students-as-teachers/

24 Opening doors to teaching: understanding the profession

Jonas Langner[1] and Andrea Zhok[2]

1. Introduction

Over the past five years, final year students in the School of Modern Languages at the University of Bristol (UoB) have had the opportunity to take our unit 'Teaching Modern Languages as a Foreign Language' for credits. The unit is currently offered for students of French, German, Italian and Spanish and taught by language teaching experts from all four languages. It was initially set up for students of German only, but due to popular demand, it was opened up to other students within the School in 2011. The unit attracts around 40 students each year and combines lectures and seminars on theoretical aspects of language teaching pedagogy with tutorials and teaching experience in local schools. This enables students to gain various transferable skills and invaluable insight into teaching as a possible future career.

Keywords: experiential learning, practical experience, MFL pedagogy, becoming a teacher.

2. What we did

For many students taking our course there is a strong element of continuity in their encounter with teaching. A significant number will have spent their year abroad (Y3) working as foreign language assistants.

1. University of Bristol, Bristol, United Kingdom; j.o.langner@bristol.ac.uk

2. University of Bristol, Bristol, United Kingdom; a.zhok@bristol.ac.uk

How to cite this chapter: Langner, J., & Zhok, A. (2016). Opening doors to teaching: understanding the profession. In E. Corradini, K. Borthwick and A. Gallagher-Brett (Eds), *Employability for languages: a handbook* (pp. 165-169). Dublin: Research-publishing.net. http://dx.doi.org/10.14705/rpnet.2016.cbg2016.479

Students with prior teaching experience take our course because they intend to gain a more structured and professional understanding of language pedagogy.

For others, however, this is the first opportunity to establish if teaching is something they feel comfortable with, and our unit aims to equip them with all the necessary knowledge and understanding – including considerations about teaching English as a foreign language – to allow them to decide whether it is a worthwhile professional option for them.

The course, spanning twelve weeks, aims to provide a thorough overview of current language pedagogy. Assessment consists of a 3,000-word essay on a theoretical issue and a reflective lesson plan detailing a 50-minute language lesson in a teaching and learning context of choice.

The presence of an in-built mandatory practical element is of special consequence in terms of making students reflect on the actual job of teaching in an Experiential Learning (EL) approach. In line with Kolb's (1984) notion of EL as "the process whereby knowledge is created through the transformation of experience" (p. 38), our unit encourages students to go through the cycle of the four EL stages, which Kolb (1984) identifies as Concrete Experience, Reflective Observation, Abstract Conceptualisation and Active Experimentation.

In week eight, tutors arrange for students to observe a language class either at a secondary school or a class offered at the UoB as part of the Applied Foreign Language programme. Students are asked to engage thoroughly with this task with the aid of a dedicated observation sheet so that all the relevant aspects of a lesson can be identified and appreciated. Students then meet their tutors and discuss what they have observed. In week nine, students need to liaise with the school-teachers, negotiate a suitable topic and seek their tutors' approval for their lesson plan. In week ten, they are required to co-teach with a fellow student part of a lesson with the class they have observed. Finally, after their teaching, they receive in-depth and specific feedback from their tutor, who will have observed them teaching.

There is a lot of feedback for students to absorb. The opportunity to observe, then plan and deliver their own lesson is extremely valuable as it forms the basis for tutors to identify concrete examples of what worked and what did not, and refers students back to issues previously dealt with in the course of the unit which now become real and personal to the students who experience them in practice. Moreover, all this forms the material for the assessed Lesson Plan (LP), where students look critically at what has happened and learn from their respective successes and mistakes. Here students have to bring together all the theoretical knowledge of language teaching pedagogy they have acquired over the course of the unit and apply it to a chosen teaching scenario. This allows the tutors to see whether students can put the theory into practice and if they have learned from their own teaching experience as well as the feedback they received for it.

This piece of assessment is very different from what students are used to, but a bespoke set of marking criteria and guidance in lectures and tutorials inform students of our expectations. The LP needs to illustrate an innovative and stimulating lesson for the chosen group of learners, using suitable aims and objectives and appropriate methods. Students also need to justify and analyse the content and material used, as well as suggest how the success of the lesson could be assessed or evaluated.

The 3,000-word essay, on the other hand, analyses one aspect of language teaching in more depth and can focus on topics such as the use of social media for language teaching and the use of L1 in the classroom.

3. Discussion of outcomes

Anecdotal evidence shows that students who took the course found it useful in preparing them for the challenges of Initial Teacher Training (ITT). The opportunity to work in schools often gives our students a vital link with the profession and with practitioners who can informally act as mentors. Some students maintain the connection with their school after they have completed the unit. This gives them a chance to do voluntary work, which often is very valuable to them to strengthen their CVs and their chances to be accepted on their ITT programme of choice. The recent Green Paper "Fulfilling our Potential" (Department for Business Innovation and Skills, 2015) on English Higher Education stresses the need to "provide greater focus on [graduate] employability" (p. 8), and this unit has proven to be an extremely useful experience for students going into teaching after graduation.

In broader terms, the unit also entails a range of transferable – hard as well as soft – skills, such as planning, negotiating (with peers, tutors and professionals), managing time, prioritising, presenting, working as part of a team, adapting quickly to new circumstances, etc. Students need to receive and process information quickly from their university tutors and also to mediate with the schools in order to make their lesson appropriate and effective. According to the latest Higher Education Academy UK Engagement Survey, students have reported that these employability skills are underdeveloped compared to "thinking critically and analytically" as part of their degree (Buckley, 2015, p. 4).

For the future, we plan to gather more quantitative data on establishing actual links with employment and/or further study after graduation. Qualitative data collected through questionnaires and focus groups would allow us to get a clearer understanding of the transferable skills students have acquired by attending this unit and engaging with the practical element of it.

4. Conclusion

Teaching, together with translating, is probably one of the employment options most closely associated with a Modern Foreign Languages degree, or at least one where the language skills acquired are an intrinsic part of the profession in question. Yet, British undergraduate language degree programmes do not systematically offer students opportunities to facilitate the transition to postgraduate study and a teaching career.

With our unit, we have set out to attempt to bridge this gap by providing a balance of theoretical and practical knowledge aimed at those students wanting to pursue a teaching profession, so that they can make informed decisions about their future in the employment market.

References and links

Buckley, A. (2015). *UKES. Students' perceptions of skills development.* Higher Education Academy. Retrieved from https://www.heacademy.ac.uk/sites/default/files/ukes_2015.pdf

Department for Business Innovation and Skills. (2015). *Fulfilling our potential: teaching and excellence, social mobility and student choice. November 2015.* London: Department for Business Innovation & Skills. Retrieved from https://www.gov.uk/government/uploads/system/uploads/attachment_data/file/474227/BIS-15-623-fulfilling-our-potential-teaching-excellence-social-mobility-and-student-choice.pdf

Kolb, D. (1984). *Experiential learning: experience as the source of learning and development.* Englewood Cliffs: Prentice Hall.

25 Leadership and languages: inspiring young linguists

Rachel Hawkes[1] and Sarah Schechter[2]

Abstract

The Language Leader Award, created by Rachel Hawkes and run by Routes into Languages East "helps pupils learn to lead, using language teaching as the medium. Throughout the year-long programme they develop their leadership and [linguistic] skills, growing in confidence and enhancing their future careers" (Hawkes, n.d. c, p. 1). Some schools use the award as an enrichment activity and others as part of the curriculum. The development of teaching skills underpins this case study which explores general themes, such as lesson planning, as well as more specific ones, such as micro-teaching and peer and teacher feedback (Hawkes, n.d. a). The students, in pairs or trios, prepare and teach at least three one-hour sessions to pupils, usually at their feeder primary schools. So far this year there are 745 students (mostly, though not exclusively, Year 9s) from 39 schools on the award programme.

Keywords: leadership, teaching, training, vocational, aspirational, reflection, practice, teamwork.

1.   Context and rationale

The project was conceived and developed in response to a perceived need to develop students' leadership skills, whilst improving their language skills. It

1. Comberton Academy Trust, Comberton, United Kingdom; rhawkes@catrust.co.uk

2. Routes into Languages East, Cambridge, United Kingdom; sarah.schechter@anglia.ac.uk

How to cite this chapter: Hawkes, R., & Schechter, S. (2016). Leadership and languages: inspiring young linguists. In E. Corradini, K. Borthwick and A. Gallagher-Brett (Eds), *Employability for languages: a handbook* (pp. 171-180). Dublin: Research-publishing.net. http://dx.doi.org/10.14705/rpnet.2016.cbg2016.480

contextualises learning by motivating students and giving them confidence and satisfaction from sharing their knowledge with others. Moreover, research has shown that knowledge is deeper when active learning occurs and is subsequently analysed, reflected upon and applied (Anderson & Krathwohl, 2001).

2.   Aims and objectives

The main aim was to provide a model within which students would develop their generic communication and leadership skills and their language learning would be rewarded, given a purpose and contextualised. Whilst developing a better understanding of the role of the teacher, they would gain a better understanding of themselves as learners. This in turn would enhance their self-esteem and confidence, improve their evaluative and analytical skills and increase their personal attainment in the target language (Hawkes, n.d. a). Reflective practice is a core aspect of the course and students record their experiences, reflections and reactions together with details of leadership activity in the school-specific logbook produced by Routes into Languages East.

3.   What we did

The project was first run on a very small scale, by its creator and developer, Rachel Hawkes, at Comberton Village College and has since grown to this year involve 745 students in 39 schools around the country. The project was set up to replicate as far as possible an authentic vocational setting, and students begin the process by completing an application form (see Figure 1).

The teacher selects the cohort and notifies Routes East so that logbooks can be provided.

Learners develop their teaching skills and prepare lessons to teach to younger learners through a series of sessions that occur during a suggested period from September to May in the academic year.

Figure 1.   Language Leader application form

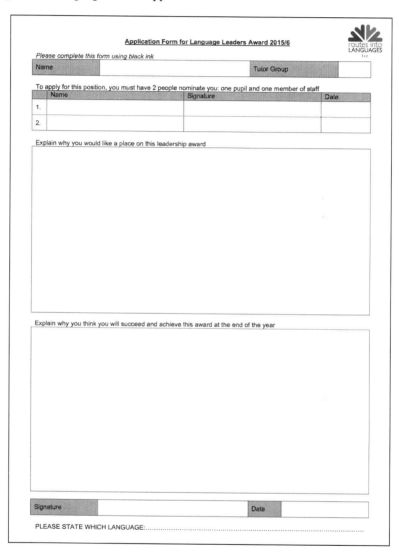

The course begins with a series of sessions offering support with lesson plans and preparation to students. This is usually – though not exclusively – carried out in the school's feeder primary schools, thus providing a valuable transition link between the two levels for both staff and students. The sessions especially focus on micro-teaching and teacher feedback. Students enrolled on the Language Leader Award course are expected to spend 25-30 hours on the course. During this time, students are offered progressive feedback and assessment, one hour of delivery with a class of younger school pupils, and the expert advice of Modern Foreign Language (MFL) teachers on various aspects of pedagogy (i.e. initial teacher training mentor). This latter phase usually takes the structure of three 20 minute sessions delivered in groups of three students, or alternatively two 20 minute sessions in pairs.

The course is delivered by teachers in schools and while they have their own schedules, they are required to include the key elements of the Award outlined in the Award Course Overview (see below Appendix 1), for example, lesson preparation, delivery, teacher body language, reflection and discussion of language and teaching issues.

The logbook is individualised for each school and is a key part of the process, with students recording their reflections and self-evaluation of each individual lesson delivered in response to directed open questions:

- How well do you feel that the lesson objective was fulfilled?

- What went well in the lesson?

- What will you do differently next time?

- How well did you work together as a team?

They chronicle their language commitment in terms of language leader activities undertaken and record supervisor feedback, and on completion of the award, they reflect on what skills they have developed as Language Leaders, what they enjoyed most and what they found most challenging. Following valuable feedback from a local teacher, Jen Turner, the logbook was updated to its present form.

On completion of the award and the logbook, the final page, with supervisor's final summative comments and confirmation that the student has shown commitment through regular attendance at language leader sessions, has completed the logbook to a high standard and has successfully delivered at least one hour of class tuition, is signed by both the supervisor and the Head Teacher (to help raise the profile of the project, languages in general, and language activity in the school). The signed slips are sent to Routes into Languages East and all successful students receive Language Leader Award certificates and lapel pins.

4.   Discussion and conclusion

The project has been extremely well received, with both teachers and students (in the primary and secondary schools) extolling its virtues. The supervisors' summative comments provide valuable insights into the process and outcomes. In giving students an insight into the pedagogic realities of teaching, they gain empathy with their teachers and, at the very least, realise the exigencies of the job and how much work goes into delivering a good lesson. On the other hand, teachers often express how much they themselves have learnt from the students and the often surprising benefits. Georgina Jackson from Tudor Grange Academy, Solihull wrote, "Emma [...] has drawn on her knowledge from other subjects and used her personal interests (history) to improve the provision of KS3 in MFL". So it is having cross-curricular benefits as well as the more obvious vocational, linguistic, aspirational and leadership ones. Although the main languages taught are French, Spanish and German (in that order), there are a range of other languages taught too, including Chinese, Russian and Welsh.

The project is growing in popularity year on year and two new projects have been developed from it and are being piloted this year. The first, Project Polyglot, by Jennifer Meechan of Hitchin Girls' School, supported by Routes into Languages East, has been awarded a British Award. It involves a cascading model, based on the Routes into Languages East Language Leader Award, with teacher training in languages for final year and second year Cambridge

University students as well as Year 12 and 10 secondary school pupils. The undergraduates and Year 12s are taught through a blended learning model with two initial input sessions together at Cambridge University and Hitchin Girls' School (with undergraduates and sixth-formers being taught together) and then with subsequent support on MOODLE. Meanwhile, the Year 10s follow the Language Leader Award. The final year undergraduates teach the Year 12s a university module topic that links to one of the A level cultural module topic areas (this will be further developed by the teacher), and the second year undergraduates teach a university module topic that can be linked to one of the five General Certificate of Secondary Education (GCSE) topic areas of the Year 10s. The Year 12s teach the Year 8s cross curricular cultural lessons of their choice in the target language. Next year the second year undergraduates will continue their involvement with the year 10s via a blog, sharing the experience with them, during their Year Abroad as part of the Routes into Languages East Adopt a Class project.

Through a combination of interactive sessions, independent work, and online support, the undergraduates will develop their teaching skills and prepare language lessons to teach to younger learners at Hitchin Girls' School in Hertfordshire. As with the Language Leader Award, the course involves micro-teaching and peer and teacher feedback. All four groups of trainees have been supplied with bespoke Routes into Languages Project Polyglot logbooks. The undergraduates will also complete a written evaluation to reflect on their experience of Project Polyglot. This will help to inform our assessment of the pilot project.

The second project to be piloted this year, the Silver Award, was developed in response to teachers in a local school whose students had completed the Language Leader Award. The project had been so successful that they – and the students – wanted to continue in some way. Usually we recommend that students progress onto the Routes into Languages South East Gold Award. However, at this particular school, they do the Language Leader Award with their Year 8s and the Gold Award includes a work placement abroad which their students are too young for, and so they required something similar and challenging, but different. Together we developed the Silver Award, which is now being piloted with seven students at the school. It is based on the Routes into Languages East Languages Challenge, developed by Vincent Everett of Northgate High School, Dereham, but the challenges are directly linked to the students' further development and improvement of their teaching and linguistic skills and aim to equip them for a more proactive language leadership role within the school. There are 27 challenges and students need to successfully complete activities worth 100 points. Their task selection is determined by personal interest and practical constraints (see Table 1).

Table 1.   Silver award challenges

TASK	POINTS
Keep your teaching from the Language Leader Award going – reflect on what you learnt from the Language Leader Award and further develop it with, for example more target language teaching.	20
Run a language festival or event in your school.	20
Investigate why languages are useful and important and run a 'Why Study Languages?' assembly for Year 9s.	20
Run a successful languages club or event or a Year 7 Spelling Bee club. Reflect as you go along on what works and what doesn't and adapt your planning accordingly.	20
Experiment with different techniques for learning vocabulary.	5
Produce a grammar guide. Use it to help other people and get feedback on how helpful it was and adapt it accordingly.	10
Create computer resources for language learning. Demonstrate them to your class.	20
Create a language-learning board/card game. Think about the target age, etc. Present the game, play it with a target age group and make sure it works. Evaluate the response.	10
Create a children's book in your target language.	10
On a trip abroad (either with the school or on a family visit) ensure you try and have as many conversations in the target language as possible and keep a record of them and the language you learn and what you notice that is different to England about the way of life and the different way of doing things.	10

Students keep evidence (photographic, videos or writing) of each task in a portfolio and then write a self-evaluation explaining what they have achieved and what they have learnt for each task. They will then choose one of their outcomes to be performed, shown or presented to parents and visitors at the

Silver Award Celebration Event at the end of the academic year. If the pilot projects are successful, they may be offered more widely as part of the Routes into Languages East standard programme.

References and links

Anderson, L. W., & Krathwohl, D. R. (2001). A taxonomy for learning, teaching and assessing: a revision of Bloom's taxonomy. New York: Longman Publishing.

Hawkes, R. (n.d. a). Language leaders award. Retrieved from http://www.rachelhawkes.com/RPP/LangLead/Overview%20of%20the%20Award.doc

Hawkes, R. (n.d. b). The award course overview document. Retrieved from http://www.rachelhawkes.com/RPP/LangLead/Language%20Leader%20Award%20Course.doc

Hawkes, R. (n.d. c). Student leadership. Retrieved from http://rilanguageleaderaward.wikispaces.com

Routes into Languages East Adopt a Class: https://www.routesintolanguages.ac.uk/events/adopt-class-1

Routes into Languages East Languages Challenge: https://routesintolanguages.ac.uk/east/activity/2682

Routes into Languages East Language Leader Award: https://www.routesintolanguages.ac.uk/events/language-leader-award-1

Routes into Languages South Gold Award: https://www.routesintolanguages.ac.uk/events/gold-award-languages-2

Appendix 1.

Language Leader Award Course Overview[3]	
Week	**Activity**
Autumn Term	
1	1. Put themselves at front of the room and address the class and introduce themselves. 2. Concentrate on eye contact, body language, movement, gestures, smiling. 3. Peer feedback and improvement the 2nd time around.

---

3. Hawkes, n.d. b, republished with kind permission of the author.

2	1. Students repeat Week 1's activity after having been given the week to observe their teachers closely in their lessons. 2. Brainstorm the qualities of an excellent teacher.
3	1. Discuss how to gain the attention of learners (in the target language). 2. Practise this with the group and take peer feedback. 3. Begin to brainstorm a list of classroom language needed (to be continued during the week by all leaders).
4	1. Share the lists of target language produced by all leaders. 2. Practise in small groups using this language and other leaders responding to it. 3. Peer feedback and improvements 2nd time around.
5	Vocal workshop to focus on projection, volume, tone of voice as well as how to use your voice better and protect it.
6	1. Introduction to the idea of structure of a lesson. 2. Discussion of different task types and the nature of each. 3. Brainstorming list of essential things to consider when planning a lesson.
7	1. Tasks and activities for the introduction of new language. 2. Teacher models some of these first (hyperlink List of Activities for the Introduction of new language). 3. Learners practise and receive peer feedback.
8	1. Learners select their theme (in groups of 3). 2. Begin to plan a first 5-minute teaching slot.
9	Leaders continue to plan their teaching.
10	Leaders micro-teach and receive peer feedback.
11	Leaders extend their planning to a full lesson (each leader responsible for 20 or 30 minutes independent delivery BUT the whole hour must cohere so they must plan together).
12	Leaders continue to work on their lesson preparation.
13	Leaders continue to work on their lesson preparation.
14	Leaders continue to work on their lesson preparation.
Spring Term	
1	Leaders teach their lessons to their peer group and receive feedback.
2	Leaders teach their lessons to their peer group and receive feedback.
3	Leaders go to primary schools and teach their lessons.
4	Leaders reflect on their Lesson 1 and write up these reflections.
5	Leaders begin to plan Lesson 2 (returning to their original notes on tasks, activities, target language lists, etc.).
6	Leaders continue to work on their lesson preparation.
7	Leaders continue to work on their lesson preparation.
8	Leaders continue to work on their lesson preparation.
9	Leaders continue to work on their lesson preparation.
10	Leaders continue to work on their lesson preparation.

11	Leaders go to primary schools and teach their lessons.
12	Leaders reflect on their Lesson 1 and write up these reflections.
Summer Term	
1	Leaders begin to plan Lesson 2 (returning to their original notes on tasks, activities, target language lists, etc.).
2	Leaders continue to work on their lesson preparation.
3	Leaders continue to work on their lesson preparation.
4	Leaders continue to work on their lesson preparation.
5	Leaders continue to work on their lesson preparation.
6	Leaders continue to work on their lesson preparation & teach their lesson to their peers.
7	Leaders continue to work on their lesson preparation & teach their lesson to their peers.
8	Leaders continue to work on their lesson preparation & teach their lesson to their peers.
9	Leaders teach their 3rd lesson.
10	Leaders reflect on their lesson and what they have learnt during the Language Leader course and record this in their Log Book.

26 The age of the monolingual has passed: multilingualism is the new normal

Bernardette Holmes[1]

1. My personal story in languages

From the first moment at the age of seven, when I picked up a second-hand picture book called *Das Braune Hühnchen und die weite, weite Welt* (which, if my memory serves me well was a Pixi Buch Nummer 15), I believe that becoming a teacher of languages was simply a matter of time. Although I didn't speak German then, it was a magical story, and I set about trying to work out from the pictures and the words that looked similar to English, exactly what was happening to the little brown hen in her blue and white-spotted dress, carrying her rolled umbrella, as she marched out bravely to discover the wide, wide world.

In the County Grammar School for Girls, it was not possible to study sciences and languages after the age of fourteen. This was a turning point. I gave up Physics to study German and Chemistry to study Latin. French was part of our core curriculum. I specialised in languages at A Level and added Ancient Greek and Ancient History, going on to read Latin and French at University.

There were a number of career paths which beckoned me, including the Foreign Office, but after a year abroad as a Foreign Languages Assistant in a huge Lycée d'Etat with over 2000 pupils, I was hooked. I had a passion for languages and literature, which combined with my experience of living through another culture during my year abroad, persuaded me that I should teach languages to other young people and offer them the same opportunities that I had been given. I believe that learning languages and spending a year abroad shaped my life, helping me to define my own identity and future path.

1. Director CLERA (Cambridge Language Education and Research Associates), Cambridge, United Kingdom; bernardette.holmes@clera.org.uk

How to cite this chapter: Holmes, B. (2016). The age of the monolingual has passed: multilingualism is the new normal. In E. Corradini, K. Borthwick and A. Gallagher-Brett (Eds), *Employability for languages: a handbook* (pp. 181-187). Dublin: Research-publishing.net. http://dx.doi.org/10.14705/rpnet.2016.cbg2016.481

I have enjoyed a very wide-ranging career in languages education as a teacher, adviser, inspector, teacher educator, researcher, curriculum developer and policy adviser. I have worked in schools, universities and for government departments. It has been a privilege to work on various iterations of the National Curriculum for Languages since its inception, playing a central role in articulating the pedagogy and support structures needed for coherent development of language learning in primary and secondary schools. My recent research interests in employability and working with employers during the Born Global project (see Notes on text at the end) has only strengthened my conviction that language capability and intercultural competence are essential elements in the personal, academic and cultural development of all young people.

The most important thing now for all teachers working with the new curriculum documents and new specifications is to read between the lines. The lack of prescription of specific content gives every teacher the opportunity to develop a programme of learning that will inspire young people to be curious, to explore the world around them and to think differently. Sharing songs, stories, and films across cultures, asking and answering questions about your own and other's lives from the earliest stages, making connections, virtual and real, with other people, and developing a greater understanding of what it is to be 'born global' will equip our young people to face the many challenges that will lie ahead, in the hope of finding fresh solutions to some of the seemingly intractable problems that we face. Willingness to be open to other languages and cultures are a defining characteristic of global education for the 21st century, transforming the way we see the world and the way the world sees us.

2. Languages today – how are languages used and how proficient do we need to be?

Findings from Born Global show that while English may be the predominant language of global business, it is certainly not the only language deployed in dealing with international clients. In larger transnational organisations and in

Small to Medium-sized Enterprises (SMEs), a wide range of other languages are used. Every language is an asset.

The most commonly spoken languages across enterprises of all sizes in the UK are French, German and Spanish, the languages of our major trading partners. Larger companies have access to native speakers of Mandarin Chinese, Italian, Arabic, Russian and Japanese in their global teams, and there is some use of languages from the newer markets such as Brazilian Portuguese, Turkish and Hindi. Companies that have been involved in recent offshoring of elements of their global business say that they are using the languages of the new locations such as Bahasa Indonesian and Bahasa Malay.

In contrast, SMEs that are actively using languages to run their business tend to be using languages from the community, like Polish and Bulgarian, in addition to the most widely used languages, French, German and Spanish. Among the participating SMEs in the Born Global survey, there is currently the same small proportion of SMEs using Lithuanian, as there are SMEs using Mandarin Chinese. This is an indication of the rich diversity of languages spoken in our local communities.

In predicting the language needs of the future, seven out of ten employers from the larger companies in the survey call for Mandarin Chinese. Close to five out of ten call for Spanish and close to four out of ten identify Arabic as one of the top three most useful languages to extend business opportunities in the future. The SMEs prioritise French, German and Spanish, as they seek to strengthen their international operations within the European Union. There is also a growing demand for Mandarin Chinese from SMEs interested in new languages with one in five saying that more speakers of Mandarin Chinese would be helpful for economic growth. The reality is that there can be *just in time* demand for a whole range of different languages, as technology connects businesses to potential clients worldwide through the internet.

Employers believe that language skills add value in a number of ways. Employers report that languages in addition to English are used internally and externally.

The current labour force is multilingual and culturally diverse, so conversations which involve more than one language take place normally between colleagues who share each other's language(s). Often colleagues are working in virtual global networks. Sharing a language can help to sustain those networks and help them to work more effectively.

The areas of external professional activity where language skills are most helpful are in building new client relationships and in strengthening existing client relationships. Using a client's language builds rapport and trust. A great deal of professional activity in all sectors of employment relies on leveraging relationships. When clients come from a different language community, if a company can connect using a common language, this adds to their credibility and to their competitive advantage. Contracts can be won or lost on an organisation's ability to speak the client's language and understand a client's culture.

Phatic skills at basic and intermediate level (CEFR A1 - B1[2]) are of value as they can break the ice and connect people through social conversation about familiar and personal matters. The simple remarks in the carpark about the weather; the exchange of sports news in the lift; the family introductions told by sharing photos on Facebook over coffee, all add value to establishing new client relationships, if they are conducted in the client's language.

Serious negotiation at boardroom level, or presentations of business strategy or running seminars about sector specific knowledge require far higher levels of fluency (CEFR B2 - C1, as a minimum with the need for C2 competence in many instances).

Reading skills are important. The ability to skim a company document for gist or read market research reports in advance of a meeting in the original language

---

2. Common European Framework of Reference for Languages: Learning, Teaching and Assessment (CEFR), available at www.coe.int/lang-CEFR. The CEFR describes language proficiency at six levels: A1 and A2, B1 and B2, and C1 and C2. The CEFR is available in 39 different languages.

deepens the understanding of a company's values and cultural norms. Those with language skills can access a broader research base and are not forced to limit their business interactions to those organisations that can speak English.

Employers recognise that a graduate with languages skills and cultural competence adds value to their organisation.

3. Languages 2020 - 2030

In a world where one in four people speaks English and the other three out of four are likely to be learning English, it would be disingenuous to suggest that speaking English as the global language is anything other than a significant asset now and for the future.

Technology makes it possible and pragmatic to choose a global language, and there are significant advantages in the use of English as the lingua franca to the knowledge economy, global research, international diplomacy and business. Yet, to the generation of young people who can be described as 'born global', living in a hyper-connected, diverse and mobile society, speaking only one language can never be regarded as enough.

To achieve personal, academic and professional goals to a global standard will require a global mind-set, an international outlook and cultural agility. These attributes are more likely to be fostered in a person who has stepped beyond the confines of the first language; the person who can see the world through another lens; the person who can read the world's history in its original languages; the person who can mediate between cultures; the person who can successfully connect to another culture using another language. English as the lingua franca will take you so far along the way, but the journey continues through other languages.

Whilst technology enables us to connect across geographical borders and time zones and the use of English facilitates international communication, analytics of internet use[3] show other languages are increasing their share of internet traffic. Cyberspace will become as multilingual as the high street, and technology, rather than promoting a monolingual, homogenous environment, opens the door to cultural diversity and the prospect of multilingual exchange. Working globally will require an understanding of an ever-widening range of languages and cultures, as we expand into different markets. Diversity means that we must represent the clients we serve.

Globalisation grows commensurate to trade liberalisation. This enables companies to outsource or offshore elements of their production in different parts of the world. When they do this, they invest in infrastructure and build up operations in different countries, recruiting highly skilled multilingual teams made up of local recruits and international recruits. While English may be used to connect groups in different countries and may be used as the lingua franca in multilingual teams, day-to-day operations are normally done local-to-local, using a local language. There will be as many languages used in global companies as there are locations and even more languages in use relative to the language and cultural profile of the client base.

The recruits of the future will require hybrid skill sets. They will need sector specific knowledge, international experience and a range of transversal employability skills such strategic leadership skills, problem-solving, global client management skills and commercial awareness. All of these skills are associated with human relations and these are developed through global communication skills in a range of languages. The age of the indulged monolingual has passed. Multilingualism is the new normal.

Notes on text

Bernardette Holmes is principal researcher of the Born Global project (http://www.britac.ac.uk/policy/Born_Global.cfm). Born Global is a major policy

---

3. Internet World Users by Language Copyright 2014 Miniwatts Marketing Group, retrieved from http://www.internetworldstats.com/stats7.htm.

research project which forms an integral part of the British Academy's Languages and Quantitative Skills Programme. It builds on previous research into the demand and supply of language skills in the UK.

The project sets out to elicit new knowledge about the extent and nature of language needs for employment to inform government language policy development and implementation.

The research aims to develop a deeper understanding of how language is used in professional contexts and how language needs are met.

It explores employers' attitudes towards language skills, recruitment and remuneration behaviours and their expectations of language competence and use.

A central purpose of the exercise is to bring forward current evidence about the value of language skills to organisations and to individuals, and, in particular, to evaluate the contribution of language skills to employability and to career progression.

At a time of significant policy reform, the report captures employers' views about the relevance of language capability to future economic growth and to the development of education and skills for the current and next generations.

Author index

19993569R00124

Printed in Great Britain
by Amazon